Living for Christ in a Fallen World

Ephesians

This inductive Bible study is designed for individual, small group, or classroom use. A leader's guide with full lesson plans and the answers to the Bible study questions is available from Regular Baptist Press. Order RBP1676 online at www.regularbaptistpress.org, e-mail orders@rbpstore.org, call toll-free 1-800-727-4440, or contact your distributor.

REGULAR BAPTIST PRESS
1300 North Meacham Road
Schaumburg, Illinois 60173-4806

The King James Version is the English translation used in our Sunday School curriculum.

The Doctrinal Basis of Our Curriculum
A more detailed statement with references is available upon request.

- The verbal, plenary inspiration of the Scriptures
- Only one true God
- The Trinity of the Godhead
- The Holy Spirit and His ministry
- The personality of Satan
- The Genesis account of creation
- Original sin and the fall of man
- The virgin birth of Christ
- Salvation through faith in the shed blood of Christ
- The bodily resurrection and priesthood of Christ
- Grace and the new birth
- Justification by faith
- Sanctification of the believer
- The security of the believer
- The church
- The ordinances of the local church: baptism by immersion and the Lord's Supper
- Biblical separation— ecclesiastical and personal
- Obedience to civil government
- The place of Israel
- The pretribulation rapture of the church
- The premillennial return of Christ
- The millennial reign of Christ
- Eternal glory in Heaven for the righteous
- Eternal torment in Hell for the wicked

LIVING FOR CHRIST IN A FALLEN WORLD: EPHESIANS
Adult Bible Study Book
Vol. 55, No. 1
© 2006
Regular Baptist Press • Schaumburg, Illinois
www.regularbaptistpress.org • 1-800-727-4440
Printed in U.S.A.
All rights reserved
RBP1679 • ISBN: 978-1-59402-369-9

Contents

Preface

The culture wars are heating up! It seems the Devil has strategically positioned anti-Christian forces in influential roles in an attempt to snuff out our Christian witness. These forces pervade university professorships, government chambers, newsrooms, and judicial courts. They team up to oppose genuine Christianity, alleging that we are narrow-minded exclusivists with divisive beliefs. They seem to thrive on the conviction that every reference to the Bible and every symbol of Christianity should be removed from public places.

For example, creationism and Intelligent Design are maligned as unacceptable religious views, whereas evolution is advanced as science. Even the word "theory" is being struck from the phrase "the theory of evolution" before it gets into textbooks.

How much longer will we be able to share the truth that God saves sinners by grace alone through faith in Jesus Christ? Many politicians, media reporters, teachers, and judges call such teaching judgmental and inappropriate. But we call it truth, and the Bible implores us to make this truth known.

By God's grace we win the culture wars one battle at a time, but we must seize each opportunity to represent Christ daily and clearly. As Paul explained to the Ephesians, believers enjoy abundant blessings but bear a great responsibility to live righteously in every relationship. We must talk about our Savior's power to save, but we must also serve as examples of our message.

As you study this series of lessons, may your appreciation of what you have in Christ deepen, and may your effectiveness for Him increase!

Count Your Blessings!

Believers thank God for salvation
by leading holy lives.

Ephesians 1:1–5

"Blessed be the God and Father of our Lord Jesus Christ, who hath blessed us with all spiritual blessings in heavenly places in Christ" (Ephesians 1:3).

P icture it—a star football running back scores his third touchdown in a playoff game. While the fans scream their appreciation, the player autographs the ball and hands it to a physically challenged boy in a nearby wheelchair section. The player has made that event a time the boy will never forget. As long as he lives, the boy will surely cherish the moment the running back singled him out of the crowd and gave him a prized possession.

The apostle Paul's letter to the Ephesians focuses on God's grace revealed to us in the gift of salvation and the many spiritual benefits that accompany it. Each of us probably remembers the day we trusted in Christ, and we should always cherish the blessings we possess because of Him.

Getting Started

1. Has someone you greatly admired honored you? If so, what was the honor?

9

2. How has that honor affected your life?

Searching the Scriptures

A Word about Ephesus

Asia, the world's largest continent, covers more than seventeen million square miles and is home to 60 percent of the world's population. In New Testament times, the name "Asia" referred to the western one-third of what we know as Turkey. At one time Asia was part of Asia Minor. Many Greeks settled there, and for a while it resembled a second Greece. Later the Romans conquered the country and made it part of the Roman Empire.

Ephesus, the largest city in the province of Asia and also its capital, was situated on the main thoroughfare between the East and the West. Because it became a great trading city, people from across the Near East settled there, causing it to become quite cosmopolitan. Jews and Gentiles rubbed shoulders in the city's streets.

Although beautiful and wealthy, Ephesus was home to spiritually impoverished men and women of unbridled religious fervor. Its two most famous structures were a stadium and the temple of Diana (Artemis), located outside the city gates. The Greeks considered the temple of Diana to be one of the Seven Wonders of the World. It measured about 425 feet long and 239 feet wide and was made of dazzling marble. Its roof rested on 120 pillars, each 55 feet high.

The stadium, then the largest in the Greek world, held twenty-five thousand spectators who gathered frequently to watch races and witness wild-beast fights.

3. What contrasts do you see between your community's cultural or architectural achievements and its spiritual condition?

Paul, the Writer

After briefly visiting Ephesus to gauge future church-planting possibilities, Paul left Aquila and Priscilla to prepare the ground. However, on Paul's third missionary journey, he returned and spent several years there. In fact, he stayed in Ephesus three years (Acts 20:31), a longer time than he had spent in any other city. His letter to the Ephesian Christians is therefore warm, personal, and fraternal.

While at Ephesus, Paul baptized a dozen disciples of John the Baptist (19:1–7), spoke boldly in the synagogue about the kingdom of God (v. 8), continued his discussions in the school of Tyrannus (vv. 9, 10), performed miracles (vv. 11, 12), witnessed the conversion of many sorcerers (vv. 18, 19), saw the Word of God make inroads into many lives (v. 20), and became the object of a mass riot (vv. 23–41). He knew firsthand that the gospel infuses grace into the hearts of some who hear it but inflames evil passions in others.

Greetings

Writing around AD 60–62 from prison in Rome (Ephesians 3:1; 4:1; 6:20), Paul identified himself as an apostle of Jesus Christ (1:1). The word "apostle" means "sent one." Christ had sent Paul into the Greek and Roman world to share the gospel with others.

4. According to verse 1, to what did Paul attribute his apostleship?

5. Why would this truth help Paul maintain an attitude of gratitude while he was in prison for serving God?

6. What is true of the heart of the person who complains about serving God?

Paul addressed his letter to "the saints which are at Ephesus" (v. 1). The term "saint" designates a holy one or one set apart to God. Every believer is a saint, although not every believer acts saintly all the time. The saints in Ephesus were "faithful in Christ Jesus" (v. 1). They demonstrated their faith in Him. Paul wished the Ephesian believers grace and peace, and he cited the Father and the Lord Jesus Christ as the givers of both (v. 2).

Like the Ephesian saints, we are "in Christ" and also in a geographic location. Our "Ephesus" may be a small town, a rural village, a mid-size urban city, or a large city. Whatever we say or do in our "Ephesus" should reflect the truth that Christ lives in us.

Verses 3–14 form one unusually long, unbroken sentence in the original language. If you want to get the effect of such a sentence, take a deep breath and try to read the entire passage before you take another breath. You will quickly get an idea of how much content Paul crammed into this one sentence as he focused on some of the blessings we have from God.

God Chose Us!

Verse 3 encourages us to bless, or praise, God, because He has granted us favors, or blessings.

7. Name just five of the many blessings believers receive in Christ.

8. What does blessing God look like in the lives of believers?

Verses 4 and 5 describe two important blessings that believers enjoy in Christ. First, we see that God chose us! After we believe on Jesus Christ, we discover that God began to work on our behalf long before we believed. "Before the foundation of the world" (v. 4), God took the first step. We will never understand the mystery of how God chose us and we "chose" Him, but we cannot miss His purpose in choosing us.

9. Read Ephesians 1:4. Why did God choose us?

10. God's purpose for choosing us affects certain parts of our lives. What are those parts?

11. Does the average unbeliever see holy living as a desirable lifestyle? Explain.

Holy living is the best life a person can live. However, our world tries to sell us on what God would consider an evil lifestyle.

Peter commented on holy living in his first epistle. He wrote, "But as he which hath called you is holy, so be ye holy in all manner of conversation [way of living]; because it is written, Be ye holy; for I [God] am holy" (1 Peter 1:15, 16).

Holiness and evil are poles apart. We must abhor evil and flee temptation so we can reflect God's holiness. Further, we must heed and obey God's Word. It teaches us to walk in God's ways (Psalm 119:105, 133).

We should not think that "blamelessness" and "sinlessness" are synonyms. We will not be sinless until we see Jesus face-to-face (1 John 3:2), but we can be blameless today and every day. Being blameless means no one can legitimately accuse us of wrongdoing. Blameless believers live above reproach.

Someone observed that we should live in such a way that we would not be afraid to sell our talking parrot to the town gossip!

12. Do you believe God chose you because you deserved salvation? Explain your answer.

God Predestinated Us!

Ephesians 1:5 points out another of God's blessings. He predestinated us. "Predestinate" means "to lay out a plan ahead of time." Verse 4 ends with the words "in love"; however, it seems these words should begin verse 5. "In love" God laid out a plan whereby He would adopt us into His family (cf. Romans 8:15; Galatians 4:5). We cannot fathom such love, a love that destined Jesus to shed His blood for us, but we can appreciate such love. And we can marvel that God planned to adopt us as His children. This adoption comes "by Jesus Christ" (Ephesians 1:5).

13. What things change for a child after he or she is adopted into a family?

14. How is the adoption of a child like God's adoption of believers?

Paul's word "adoption" identifies us as full-grown, mature, responsible sons and daughters. God foreordained all of these family benefits "according to the good pleasure of his will" (v. 5).

15. Read 2 Samuel 9. Who received virtual adoption into King David's family?

16. What benefits did this "adopted son" receive from King David?

17. What similar benefits do you have because God has adopted you?

18. What divine characteristics do you see reflected in King David's treatment of the person he "adopted"?

Making It Personal

The topics of election and predestination have captivated theologians for centuries. Debates about both topics rage in Bible college and seminary classrooms and in dormitories, as well as in Sunday School classes and home Bible study groups. We may never understand all that is involved in God's choice and predestination, but we can understand clearly how God's chosen and predestined people ought to live. We should be "holy and without blame before him" (Ephesians 1:4).

19. Your thankfulness for salvation can be measured by how holy you have lived. Think about how holy your life has been. How thankful for salvation have you been?

20. Jesus prayed that the Father would "sanctify" us (make us holy) by His Word (John 17:17). How will you apply God's Word to your life this week so you will become more holy and blameless?

21. Thank God for your salvation every day this week. Plan to tell five people in person that you are thankful for your salvation. Write those fives names here. After the week is over, record how expressing verbal gratitude for your salvation affected your life.

22. Memorize Ephesians 1:3 and use it as a reminder of the blessings you have in God.

Sharing a Fabulous Inheritance

*God redeems believers and gives them
an inheritance.*

Ephesians 1:6–14

**"In whom ye also trusted, after that ye heard
the word of truth, the gospel of your salvation:
in whom also after that ye believed, ye were
sealed with that holy Spirit of promise, which
is the earnest of our inheritance until the redemption of the purchased possession, unto the
praise of his glory" (Ephesians 1:13, 14).**

Two snowbirds driving south in a luxury RV left no doubt
in the minds of other motorists about their destination.
A bumper sticker on the back of their RV announced, "Florida Bound!"
The couple also left no doubt about their attitude. A second bumper
sticker said it all: "We're spending our kids' inheritance."

Generally speaking, inheritances aren't as large as they used to
be. Senior adults are living longer and finding their Social Security
and 401(k) funds drying up as health care costs and day-to-day living
expenses increase. For every two seniors who opt to spend their children's inheritance on pleasure, there are probably hundreds who are re-
luctantly spending theirs on necessities. As a result, most people today

had better not count on receiving a windfall inheritance. Most of it will have blown away.

There is good news though. Ephesians 1:11 mentions an inheritance that we can't lose.

Getting Started

1. What have you seen that indicates senior adults are using funds they had hoped to leave to their children?

2. What are the threats to a person's nest egg, or a reserve of money?

3. What measures do people take to protect their nest eggs?

Searching the Scriptures

Ephesians 1:3 introduces Paul's tribute to God for His many blessings. He has chosen us believers (v. 4) and predestined us to be His adopted children (v. 5). In verse 6 Paul informed his readers concerning why God blesses believers.

When God made us His children, He manifested His glorious grace. The gracious acts of God that make sinners into saints bring praise to His grace. We are not saved because of our goodness; we are saved because of God's greatness and grace (2:8, 9). Simply stated, God blesses us to bring praise to Himself (Ephesians 1:6; 2 Corinthians 4:15).

Paul told the Ephesians that God has made believers "acceptable in the beloved" (Ephesians 1:6).

4. How would you react if a strange person walked into your house unannounced and uninvited?

5. How would you react if a strange person walked into your house as a guest of one of your grown children?

God did not accept us because of anything we did. In fact, because of our sin, He could not fellowship with us, call us His children, or let us enter Heaven. But because of our relationship with His Beloved Son, Jesus Christ, He has accepted us.

6. Why is it appropriate to identify Jesus Christ as the Beloved (v. 6)?

7. How should a believer respond to being accepted in the Beloved?

In Ephesians 1:7–14 Paul discussed how God blesses us in addition to being chosen (v. 4) and predestinated (v. 5) by Him.

Redemption

When we were spiritually bankrupted and condemned sinners, Jesus Christ came to our aid. He paid the penalty of sin for us (Hebrews 9:22, 26) and redeemed us at the cost of His blood (Romans 3:24; Colossians 1:12–14; Hebrews 9:12). When we accept Him as our Savior, God applies the provision of Christ to our account.

8. Read Hebrews 9:22. Why did our redemption require the shedding of Jesus' blood?

Christ's blood was the payment for our redemption (1 Peter 1:18–20). Jesus Christ voluntarily became our sin offering (cf. Isaiah 53:10; 2 Corinthians 5:21). He offered Himself vicariously. That is, He substituted His life for our lives. He died in our place. Consequently, Paul wrote, "In whom we have redemption through his blood" (Ephesians 1:7).

9. What can we gain from rehearsing in our minds what God redeemed us from?

Forgiveness

God didn't stop at redemption. When God redeemed us, He emancipated us (or set us free) from the guilt and punishment of sin (Galatians 3:13; Colossians 1:14; Titus 2:14). In simpler terms, He forgave us (Ephesians 1:7).

10. What characterizes true forgiveness?

We saints are simply sinners set free from sin's penalty and condemnation and from bondage to sin and Satan. We are not perfect, but God sees us as fully forgiven in Christ. We still have a sin nature and will have it until we get our glorified bodies at the Rapture. Because of our sin nature we still sin, and we must confess our sins to God (1 John 1:9). However, no sins that we commit after salvation would cause us to lose our standing as forgiven in God's sight. When God forgave us, He took our sins away for good (John 1:29; Romans 10:13).

11. Read Ephesians 1:7. Out of what did our redemption and forgiveness of sin spring?

12. After a believer is redeemed and forgiven, what should that person do with his or her firsthand knowledge of God's grace that redeems and forgives?

Understanding

In addition to redeeming and forgiving us according to His abundant grace, God "abounded toward us in all wisdom and prudence"

(Ephesians 1:8). He revealed truth to us, and out of His abundant grace, He enabled us to understand it.

One of the things God caused us to understand is the mystery of His will concerning the unity of Jews and Gentiles. In verses 9 and 10 Paul explained the mystery of the "dispensation of the fulness of times." The Biblical definition of "mystery" differs from our definition of the word. A Biblical mystery is not mysterious. It refers to a truth God hid in the Old Testament but revealed in the New Testament. By divine revelation we can understand such a mystery.

God revealed to the apostle Paul that in the end time He will gather under His authority all things in Heaven and on the earth (v. 10). At that time both saved Jews and saved Gentiles will participate in the millennial Kingdom. Once again, none of this divine plan depends on human merit. The establishment of the messianic Kingdom and the role of saved Jews and saved Gentiles in it is according to God's "good pleasure which he hath purposed in himself" (v. 9).

13. Read Isaiah 11:1–10. What qualities about the Millennium appeal to you the most?

14. How should an understanding about the culmination of all things in Christ affect believers?

Heirs of the King

Ephesians 1:11 declares the astonishing truth that in Christ "we have obtained an inheritance." We are "heirs of God, and joint-heirs with Christ," according to Romans 8:17. We suffer now, but someday we will be glorified (v. 18) and will reign with Christ (2 Timothy 2:12). When Jesus establishes His Kingdom on earth, He will fully restore Israel's land. God promised this land to Israel as an everlasting inheritance, but we will enjoy the fruits of Messiah's Kingdom as heirs of the King.

15. Why is certainty about a future inheritance such an attractive prospect in our world today?

In Ephesians 1:12 Paul used "we" to refer to Jews. In verse 13 he used "ye" to refer to the Gentiles. His description, "who first trusted in Christ" (v. 12) refers to Jews, for they received the gospel before Gentiles did. Then in verse 14 he used "our" to indicate both Jews and Gentiles.

Verse 11 describes Jewish believers as "being predestinated according to the purpose of him who worketh all things after the counsel of his own will." God predestinated, or marked out, Jewish believers to "be to the praise of his glory" (v. 12). He "worketh all things after the counsel of his own will" (v. 11). God decided to make Jewish believers His inheritance. God laid out the plan according to His own will, and He carried it out according to His own will. The result is that He will receive glory for sending His Son to die for sinful mankind, redeeming and forgiving sinners, making them His children, and taking them to Heaven to spend eternity with Him.

Sealed by the Spirit

Ephesians 1:13 mentions the sealing with the Holy Spirit. The phrase "after that ye believed" may be rendered "when ye believed," implying that the Holy Spirit seals the believer at the moment of salvation.

16. What would you consider to be the safest place for valuables?

17. What could happen, even in the safest place, to corrupt valuables?

18. How should knowing that the Holy Spirit is the keeper of the

believer's spiritual inheritance affect the believer's hope for the future?

According to verse 14, the sealing with the Holy Spirit serves as an earnest (token of what is to come; a pledge) of our inheritance (see 2 Corinthians 1:22). It is a down payment guaranteeing more to come (2 Corinthians 5:5).

Among other blessings, God has promised us glorified bodies at the Rapture (Romans 8:11; 1 Corinthians 15:51–54; Philippians 3:21). The sealing with the Spirit guarantees that someday God will redeem (deliver) our bodies, our "purchased possession" (Ephesians 1:14). Although God saved us when we believed, our bodies are still subject to disease and death. However, He will redeem our bodies too, and as a pledge of that promise, He has sealed us with the Holy Spirit.

19. What aspect of heavenly life in a glorified body do you find most appealing? Why?

Making It Personal

Believers enjoy a rich and enjoyable life *in* Christ now and anticipate an even better life *with* Christ forever. To what do we owe these present and future blessings? Two significant words in Ephesians 1:7 supply the answer. They are "redemption" and "grace." Jesus provided redemption for us by shedding His blood; and divine grace not only saved us but secured forgiveness and all other blessings for us. What Jesus did on our behalf in the past has a profound bearing on what God is doing for us today and on what He plans to do for us in the future.

20. How often do you contemplate your future in Christ? How would contemplating your future in Christ affect the joy you experience now?

21. How does the fact that Christ will reign on earth help you cope with

a. pain and suffering?

b. ridicule or other persecution?

c. the loss of a friend or a loved one?

d. distressing world conditions?

22. How can you describe the joy of forgiveness to an unsaved friend or loved one?

23. Memorize Ephesians 1:13 and 14. Meditate on these verses, and write a prayer to God glorifying Him for the guarantee of a wonderful inheritance.

Prayer Changes Things—and People

*God's power persuades believers
to pray confidently.*

Ephesians 1:15–23

**"Wherefore I also, after I heard of your faith in
the Lord Jesus, and love unto all the saints, cease
not to give thanks for you, making mention of
you in my prayers" (Ephesians 1:15, 16).**

L ORD, YOU KNOW MY NINTH BIRTHDAY WILL BE HERE
SOON! PLEASE GIVE ME A SKATEBOARD!
I *REALLY* NEED A SKATEBOARD!"

Troy yelled so loud his mother ran from the kitchen to his upstairs
bedroom.

Standing over her kneeling son, she advised, "Troy, the Lord isn't
hard of hearing. You don't have to shout to be heard."

"I know," Troy replied, "but I want Grandpa on the porch to hear
me too."

Like Troy, we may think the Lord needs some help to answer our
prayers. But such thinking fails to recognize His omnipotence and
promise to hear us when we call on Him in partnership with His will.

Getting Started

1. What causes people to lack confidence as they pray?

2. When have you prayed without much confidence?

Searching the Scriptures

Paul told the Ephesians he thanked God for them after he had heard reports about their faith and love (Ephesians 1:15, 16). We might find it a little strange that Paul wrote that he had "heard" of their faith and love. Hadn't he preached in Ephesus for three years? Why would he have to hear this good news from someone else? When he wrote this letter to the Ephesians, he had been absent from Ephesus for five years.

Because of the good reports, Paul could thank God for the spiritual progress of the Ephesian believers. He felt grateful that his work among them was still bearing fruit.

3. Read Ephesians 1:15. What is the relationship between faith and love? (See John 13:35.)

4. Read Ephesians 1:16. For whom did Paul give thanks? To Whom did he give thanks?

5. Why did Paul not thank the *Ephesians* for their work of love?

Consistent Prayer

Praying for believers was a consistent practice in Paul's life. He prayed for Christians at Rome (Romans 1:7, 8), at Corinth (1 Corinthians 1:2, 4), at Philippi (Philippians 1:1, 3), and at Thessalonica (1 Thessalonians 1:1, 2; 2 Thessalonians 1:1, 3).

6. According to 1 Timothy 2:1 and 2 and Ephesians 6:18, for whom should a believer pray?

7. How can a believer keep from being overwhelmed by the seemingly endless number of people to pray for?

Although Paul was an extremely busy missionary, he was never too busy to pray.

8. What ministries could Paul have accomplished instead of spending time in prayer?

9. Is heavy involvement in ministry a good excuse for skipping time in prayer? What could be the results of such a practice?

Prayer for Wisdom

In Ephesians 1:17 Paul prayed for wisdom, not for himself, but for the Ephesians. He asked that God would give them "the spirit of wisdom and revelation in the knowledge of him." What does "the spirit of wisdom and revelation" refer to? Some commentators believe it refers to the Holy Spirit. As a member of the Godhead, the Holy Spirit is all-wise. He supervised the writing of the Scriptures, the written revelation of God.

However, because the Ephesian Christians were saved, the Spirit already dwelled in them (Romans 8:9). Paul would not pray that God would give the Spirit to people who had already received Him.

In the King James Version of Ephesians 1:17, the "s" of "spirit" is not capitalized. The translators of the KJV thought that this word referred to something other than the Holy Spirit. Probably "the spirit of wisdom and revelation" refers to having a wise and discerning spirit.

This spiritual wisdom and revelation involves "the knowledge of him." Paul desired that the saints have spiritual wisdom so they could have a better acquaintance with God Himself. The goal of our lives should be to know God well. Jesus prayed, "And this is life eternal, that they might know thee the only true God, and Jesus Christ, whom thou hast sent" (John 17:3).

10. How can a believer gain an intimate knowledge of God?

Eyes of Understanding

The spirit of wisdom and revelation in the knowledge of God enlightens the mind. Paul prayed that God would enlighten "the eyes of [the Ephesians'] understanding" (Ephesians 1:18). The Holy Spirit must work within us to enlighten our minds; we cannot do it ourselves. We do not have an innate ability to know spiritual things. That's why the unsaved cannot understand spiritual truths (1 Corinthians 2:14).

In Ephesians 1:18 and 19 Paul listed three benefits of having our minds illuminated.

11. What three benefits of illumination do you find named in Ephesians 1:18 and 19?

The Hope of His Calling

"The hope of his calling" (v. 18) refers to the hope that springs from the call of God. (See Ephesians 4:1, 2 Timothy 1:9, and 1 Peter 2:9.) This hope anticipates the future, the destiny God had in mind for us when He called us.

12. Read 1 John 3:2. What hope is included in this verse?

13. Why is it important to know the hope of God's calling?

Someday the world will recognize us as children of God. At that time we, the church, will also reign with Christ and be His spotless Bride (Revelation 19:7, 9).

The Riches of His Inheritance

The second result of illuminated understanding is that we know "the riches of the glory of his inheritance in the saints" (Ephesians 1:18). The saints are God's inheritance. God looks upon believers as a treasure of incomparable worth (5:2). He receives glory through us (3:21).

14. In light of 1 Peter 2:9, why should a believer avoid a belittling view of him- or herself?

The Greatness of His Power

The third benefit of an illuminated mind is that of knowing "the exceeding greatness of his power to us-ward who believe" (Ephesians 1:19).

15. Why is the word "exceeding" in Ephesians 1:19 such an important word?

Verses 19–23 describe God's power as "working," which means "operating strongly and effectually"; "mighty," which implies forcefulness; and "power," which means "dominion and strength." In other words, God brought about our redemption through the strong, effectual operation of His forceful strength and dominion.

Paul continued to illustrate the greatness of God's power at work in our redemption by referring to two aspects of Christ's life. First, Paul compared the power that brought about our conversion to the power that raised Christ from the dead (v. 20).

16. Read Ephesians 1:20. What, if anything, is more powerful than the power to raise a person from the dead?

17. What made Christ's resurrection unique from all other resurrections up to that point in history? (See Hebrews 7:25 and 10:12.)

The power of God not only raised Jesus from the dead, but it also exalted Him to the Father's right hand (Ephesians 1:20), the place of honor and authority.

18. How should knowing the permanence of Christ's position help a believer?

19. What enormous challenges are not too great for the power of God?

God exalted Christ above all other beings—above the highest angels and far above mankind (v. 21). Jesus is the exalted head of the church (v. 22). Furthermore, someday every knee will bow before Him (Philippians 2:10).

Making It Personal

Certainly Paul knew the Lord well; but according to Philippians 3:10, he aspired to know Him better. He wanted a deeper knowledge of Christ, the power of His resurrection, and the fellowship of His sufferings. The better Paul knew God, the more he relied on Him.

20. Make a list of the burdens on your heart.

21. Reread Ephesians 1:19 and 20. Take your burdens to the Lord, making sure to state your confidence in His power to help you through them.

22. If you haven't already, make a list of people you need to pray for. Send four of those people a note letting them know that you have prayed for them this week.

23. Memorize Ephesians 1:15 and 16. Commit to the Lord to pray faithfully for others.

Saved by Grace for Good Works

*A believer's union with Christ
allows him or her to produce good works.*

Ephesians 2:1–10

"For we are his workmanship, created in Christ Jesus unto good works, which God hath before ordained that we should walk in them" (Ephesians 2:10).

As a result of improper medical treatment, hymnist Fanny J. Crosby was blind for all but the first six weeks of her ninety-four years of life. Her husband, too, was blind, and their first child died in infancy. However, Fanny Crosby had the reputation of being happy, and she became a much-sought-after public speaker.

Early in life Fanny began memorizing the Bible. Eventually she could recite Genesis through Deuteronomy, Ruth, many portions of Psalms, Proverbs, Song of Solomon, and much of the New Testament. Fanny used her familiarity with Scripture as the basis for the eight thousand gospel songs she wrote.

"Saved by Grace" may be among her best-loved songs. She wrote the words in a matter of minutes at age seventy-one after someone read her a tract. Her publisher paid her two dollars for the words, but he never printed them. After three years, Fanny used the words in an

address that she gave at a Christian workers' conference. Someone at
the conference recorded her words, and before long a noted Christian
musician provided the music. The song became one of D. L. Moody's
favorites. He used it at his evangelistic meetings.

God's grace is not just a nice topic for a song. Rather, it is a vital
part of salvation and the Christian life. In Ephesians 2:1–10 the apostle
Paul addressed God's grace.

Getting Started

1. What is your favorite song about God's grace? What makes it
your favorite?

2. How would Fanny Crosby's life have been different if she had
not viewed God's grace as an opportunity for good works?

Searching the Scriptures

Dead in Sin

In Ephesians 2:1 the apostle Paul addressed the Ephesian Gentiles
as "you." In 2:3 he referred to the Ephesian Jews as "we." He told both
groups they had been dead in trespasses and sins before God saved
them. Many who rely on good deeds for salvation overlook the fact that
they are spiritually dead. Unbelievers are not simply weakened, dis-
abled, sick, or incapacitated: they are dead in their sins.

3. What are some effects of being dead in trespasses and sins?

It's just as impossible for a sinner to work his or her way into Heav-
en as it is for a dead cowboy to star in a Wild West bronco show. A per-

son in the natural state is not in tune with God. Rather, he or she walks "according to the course of this world" (v. 2).

4. Read Ephesians 2:2. What does physical walking involve?

5. What does it mean to walk "according to the course of this world" (v. 2)?

6. What significance is seen in Satan's name, the "prince of the power of the air" (v. 2)?

Children of Disobedience and Wrath

A person in the natural state is also a child of the Devil. No wonder Paul referred to the unsaved as the "children of disobedience" (v. 2).

7. Why does the standing of unbelievers as "children of disobedience" make it impossible for them to claim that they are free to do anything?

8. How could intentionally pumping up a child's ego affect his or her receptivity to the gospel?

Before salvation, the Jewish believers had been no better off than their Gentile counterparts. Paul wrote that the Jewish Christians (including himself) had followed the lusts of the flesh and mind (v. 3). Like the Gentiles, the Jews had been dominated by their unregenerate desires, deserved God's wrath, and were in danger of it. They were "by nature the children of wrath."

9. Why is the phrase "by nature the children of wrath" important (v. 3)?

10. According to Revelation 20:12–15, what is the final destination of all those who continue under God's wrath?

11. According to Romans 8:1, why are believers safe from divine wrath?

God's Great Love

In Ephesians 2:4 and 5 Paul introduced a striking contrast between our former lost condition and our present saved condition, and he credited God with the difference. God rescued us from death and wrath and blessed us with life.

12. Read Ephesians 2:4. What motivated God to act on behalf of mankind?

13. Name someone you love dearly. Why do you love that person so much?

14. Read Ephesians 2:5. What was the condition of mankind when God chose to show His love toward us? (See Romans 5:6–8.)

Alive in Christ

Love is an intrinsic part of God's nature (1 John 4:8). God met us where we were, and He "quickened" us; that is, He gave us life (Ephesians 2:5). He made us alive spiritually by imparting the life of Christ to us. By grace He did for us what we could never do for ourselves. He saved us (v. 5).

15. Why was the message of "saved by grace" particularly important for the Jews to hear? (See Romans 2:17–24.)

In the first part of Ephesians 2:6, Paul taught that God has made us alive together with Christ, whom He raised from the dead. When the Spirit of God regenerated us, He raised us from the dead spiritually. In the future, at the Rapture, He will raise dead Christians and will also physically transform living Christians (1 Thessalonians 4:13–17). But God didn't stop with raising us from the dead spiritually and physically. He has also made us to "sit together in heavenly places in Christ Jesus" (Ephesians 2:6). Note that God has already accomplished this action. Paul wasn't referring to something that will happen in the future.

16. Since God has made us "sit together in heavenly places in Christ Jesus," how secure is a believer's salvation?

☐ tentatively secure
☐ not secure at all
☐ perfectly secure

17. How should being secure in salvation affect a believer's service for the Lord?

God's Rich Grace

Christ's resurrection also serves as the basis of all our present blessings (v. 7). God's grace that brought us salvation also floods our hearts with blessings that help us live victoriously.

18. Read Ephesians 2:7. Why is it important that the riches of God's grace toward us now are "exceeding"? (Compare 2:7 to 1:19 and 3:20.)

As God's saved sons and daughters, we should always recognize that we are blessed because God is gracious. We do not deserve any blessings. Ephesians 2:8 and 9 state, "For by grace are ye saved through faith; and that not of yourselves: it is the gift of God: not of works, lest any man should boast." Salvation comes by grace through faith. To have faith means to trust or to rely on Jesus Christ and what He did for us. When He died on the cross, He paid for our sins. In fact, He satisfied all of God's just demands for payment of the penalty for sin. To receive this forgiveness, we must trust in Him.

Not by Works

Having explained what brings about salvation, Paul contradicted what so many religious people rely on for salvation: namely, "works." All who hope to get to Heaven by being good entertain a false hope. No one can be good enough to earn his or her way to Heaven. Going to church has not saved even one soul. Giving to a church's offering has never saved a soul. Being a good husband, wife, or neighbor has never saved anyone. Paying one's bills or keeping one's promises never has saved a person. Paul wrote plainly that salvation is not of works (v. 9). We cannot earn it. God does not give it to us as a reward. We cannot buy it. We cannot work for it. Nor is it partly by faith and partly by works. It is not by works at all.

19. Read Ephesians 2:1–3 and 9. What is true of all the works of those who try to earn salvation?

If we could get to Heaven by being good enough or by doing enough good deeds, the greatest boasters of all time would inhabit Heaven. Some would boast, "I went to church every Christmas and Easter." Others would brag, "That's nothing. I went every Sunday morning, every Sunday evening, and every Wednesday night." A few would try to overshadow those accomplishments with, "I did all that and had perfect attendance in Sunday School too."

But there won't be any boasting in Heaven, because every resident will confess, "I'm here because Jesus Christ, God's Son, died on the cross to pay for my sin. I simply trusted in Him."

Scripture affirms that good works can never save us. Romans 4:5 declares, "But to him that worketh not, but believeth on him that justifieth the ungodly, his faith is counted for righteousness."

God's Eternal Purpose

20. Read Ephesians 2:10. What would you say to someone who believes God's plan for his or her life ended with salvation?

God makes it clear that He wants us to be involved in good works after we have trusted Christ as Savior. We ought to be vitally involved in a local church (Ephesians 4:11–13). We should also pray with other believers (Romans 15:30; Ephesians 6:18). We ought to be good husbands, good wives, good neighbors, and good citizens (Ephesians 5:22—6:9; Romans 13; Colossians 3:18–25). We also ought to diligently study our Bibles (2 Timothy 2:15).

We ought to do good works because we are God's children and because His Word teaches us to do these things. God's plan for our lives includes doing good works.

Making It Personal

The Bible is extremely practical. It tells us how to be saved and how to live as believers. We can be saved only by grace through faith in Christ, and we can lead godly, effective lives only by grace through faith in Christ (Galatians 2:20; Titus 2:11, 12). As the recipients of God's amazing grace, we should be gracious people and faithful servants of God.

21. If a judge were to watch a video of your life from the past week, would he or she find enough evidence to conclude you are a believer? What would that evidence be?

22. If you were to stand before a judge one week from now, what good works would you compile between now and then as evidence of your salvation?

23. Memorize Ephesians 2:10. As you work for the Lord this week, remember that you are fulfilling God's eternal purpose for your life.

The Wall Came Down

Believers are one in Christ.

Ephesians 2:11–22

"For he is our peace, who hath made both one, and hath broken down the middle wall of partition between us" (Ephesians 2:14).

What comes to your mind when you think of enormous walls? Perhaps the Great Wall of China? This wall, built in the early third century before Christ to keep foreigners out of China, stretched about 1,500 miles and had an additional 1,780 miles of buttresses. The wall averaged 25 feet in height and was 15 to 30 feet thick at the base. It took about 300,000 laborers to build it. The Chinese kept the wall in good repair until the 1600s. Over the past four decades, the Chinese have dismantled parts of the wall, including a section they blew up to make way for a dam.

Maybe you think of the infamous Berlin Wall, which Soviet soldiers and the East German police built in 1961 to keep East Germans from escaping to the West. The Berliners called it *Schandmauer,* or "wall of shame." Free people everywhere rejoiced in 1989, when the wall was torn down.

In Ephesians 2:11–22 the apostle Paul described another ancient wall, the figurative wall that separated Jews and Gentiles.

Getting Started

1. Why do people build walls or fences around their properties?

2. Would you rather live in a neighborhood of adjoining lawns or a neighborhood of fenced-in yards? Why?

3. What figurative walls do believers often erect between themselves and other believers within a local church?

Searching the Scriptures

Do you have a good memory? Can you remember what happened last Monday? a year ago today? five years ago today? The Bible uses the words "remember," "remembered," and "remembrance" about 250 times. In Ephesians 2:11 Paul challenged the Ephesians to remember their lives before God saved them by His grace. He wanted them to remember their physical lives. As "Gentiles in the flesh" (v. 11), they were uncircumcised heathen. The Jews referred to the Gentiles as the "Uncircumcision" (v. 11), implying that the Gentiles were unclean and profane.

God had instituted circumcision at the time of Abraham (Genesis 17:10, 14). This mark identified Abraham and his descendants through Isaac as His Chosen People. However, the Hebrews eventually began to look upon this sign as something that had objective power to make them righteous. This attitude continued into the first century, so Paul described circumcision as "in the flesh" and "made by hands" to emphasize that it was only an external mark (Ephesians 2:11). Paul implied that the Jews needed spiritual regeneration. But his main purpose was to remind the Gentile believers that they had been profane and unclean heathen before God's grace reached them.

The Way Things Used to Be

Paul's readers' lives changed greatly when they came to know
Christ. But Paul briefly described the way things had been (Ephesians
2:12). The portrayal applies to any unsaved person today as well.

4. According to verse 12, what five conditions characterized the
Ephesians before they trusted in Christ?

5. What one word would you use to sum up the life of every Christian before he or she became a believer?

In spite of technological advances, modern culture fares no better
than first-century culture. Our non-Christian contemporaries are as lost
as the first-century pagans. The unsaved do not know Christ, and they
have no claim to the promises God made to ancient Israel. They cannot claim any special favors from God because they were born in a so-
called Christian nation. They have "no hope, and [are] without God in
the world" (v. 12). Life is fragile, and the world resembles a powder keg
with a short fuse, but the unsaved have no genuine hope of personal
security. Without God, they are confused and lost. Their future on earth
is bleak, and eternal perdition awaits them.

6. What about a believer's past might make him or her feel superior
to other believers, especially new believers?

7. What effect should verse 12 have on believers who feel superior
to others?

What a Difference Christ Makes

Like sunshine after a dark storm, the beginning of verse 13 radiates warmth and light. By saving the Ephesians, Christ had bridged the long-standing gap that had separated Jews and Gentiles. His blood had brought far-off Gentile believers into close proximity with God and with Jewish believers.

Ephesians 2:14 declares that Christ "hath made both one." He died on the cross to make one new man from two (v. 15). Because of the work of Christ, Jewish and Gentile believers enjoy unity in Christ. "One plus one equals one" may not be good math, but it is excellent theology as it relates to the reconciling work of Christ.

8. Read Ephesians 2:14 and 15. What is the basis of peace between believers?

9. How should the designation "one new man" in Christ affect the way believers view one another today?

We are unified in Christ. Humanity includes many races, ethnic groups, and cultures. But those from different backgrounds are in Christ—all are one. Galatians 3:28 teaches the same truth: "There is neither Jew nor Greek, there is neither bond nor free, there is neither male nor female: for ye are all one in Christ Jesus."

When Christ died, He fulfilled the law. Thus He abolished "the law of commandments contained in ordinances" (Ephesians 2:15). Consequently, we believers do not live under the constraints of the law; we live in the Dispensation of Grace.

When a Jew trusts Christ as his or her Savior, that person becomes a member of the Body of Christ. Christ reconciles him or her to God. When a Gentile believes on the Lord Jesus Christ, that person, too, becomes a member of the Body of Christ and is reconciled to God. "God was in Christ, reconciling the world unto himself" (2 Corinthians 5:19). Since both have become members of the same Body, they can reconcile with each other. The enmity has gone. Christ has slain it, or done away with it. He has broken down the wall.

10. Read Ephesians 2:16. What does disunity in a local church do to the testimony of the work of the cross of Christ?

Equal Access

Christ offers peace and pardon to the Gentiles, who "were afar off," and to the Jews, who "were nigh" (Ephesians 2:17). According to verse 18, both Jewish and Gentile believers have access to God the Father through Christ by the Holy Spirit. God has opened the door of Heaven to us. We will enter Heaven someday, and we will live there forever in perfect bliss; but even now we can access Heaven through prayer. According to Hebrews 4:16, God invites us to "come boldly to the throne of grace, that we may obtain mercy, and find grace to help in time of need."

11. How can equal access to the Father through prayer serve as a unifying factor among believers?

12. Read Ephesians 6:18. How would carrying out the command in this verse help preserve unity within a local church?

In the last four verses of Ephesians 2, Paul used three metaphors to relate truth about the unity between Jewish and Gentile believers in Christ. These metaphors also serve to help believers today understand their unity with one another—particularly within a local church.

Fellow Citizens

Gentiles were seen as "strangers and foreigners" before the work of Christ made them fellow citizens with the Jewish Christians (v. 19).

13. Read Ephesians 2:19. What responsibilities do fellow citizens have to one another?

14. How do those responsibilities apply to the citizen relationship that believers have with one another in Christ?

Family Members

The second metaphor Paul used drew a closer tie between the Gentile and the Jewish believers. He referred to them as being part of the "household of God" (v. 19).

15. What responsibilities do family members have toward one another?

16. How do those responsibilities apply to the family relationship that believers have with one another in Christ?

Parts of a Building

The third metaphor is that of a building (vv. 20–22). The foundation of this building was "the apostles and prophets" (v. 20). The apostles included men such as Peter, James, and John, whom Christ chose. Paul was also considered an apostle. "The prophets" probably referred to the New Testament prophets of the first Christian generation.

The chief cornerstone of the building is Jesus Christ (v. 20). As the most important part of the building, the chief cornerstone serves as a guide for the construction of the whole building. The building, of course, is the church, which comprises all believers.

17. What are some cornerstones a church might use for direction instead of Christ?

18. How does a local church practically look to Christ as their chief cornerstone?

The Temple of God

The church is also a "holy temple in the Lord" (Ephesians 2:21). At one time God dwelled in a temple of stone constructed originally by Solomon (1 Kings 8:14–21). Now God dwells in the hearts of those who believe in Him (1 Corinthians 6:19) and in the church as a whole (3:16, 17; "ye" is plural here). Not only is God in the temple, but the temple is also in God. All who compose this building are "in Christ."

19. How does being the temple of God the Holy Spirit give believers the opportunity to realize the unity that God wants them to have? (See Ephesians 5:18–21.)

Making It Personal

No believer should erect a wall between him- or herself and another believer, because Christ died to break down such walls. Honestly consider whether you have built walls between yourself and other believers. Take the first steps in tearing down the walls: confess your sin to God and then accept the person or people you have wronged.

20. a. With whom do you need to reconcile?

  b. How will you reconcile with that person?

  c. When will you reconcile with that person?

True fellowship enjoys the closeness believers find in the Body of Christ. All believers ought to work to create this closeness.

21. Choose a believer whom you don't know very well. Plan ways to get to know that believer better this week. Record your plan below.

22. Memorize Ephesians 2:14 as a reminder of Christ's provision for unity within your local church.

The Greatest Mystery Ever Disclosed

The gospel is for all people, regardless of culture or background.

Ephesians 3:1–13

"Unto me, who am less than the least of all saints, is this grace given, that I should preach among the Gentiles the unsearchable riches of Christ; and to make all men see what is the fellowship of the mystery, which from the beginning of the world hath been hid in God, who created all things by Jesus Christ" (Ephesians 3:8, 9).

Some adults are old enough to remember when they sat by the radio and listened to mysteries such as *The Shadow* and *The Thin Man*. Other adults may recall TV episodes of *Perry Mason* and *Columbo*. It seems everyone enjoys trying to solve a well-constructed mystery. Of course no one likes having to solve such mysteries as, "Where did I leave my purse?" "How can we stretch our budget to the end of the month?" "What does the boss expect me to accomplish with so few resources and an extremely tight deadline?"

Getting Started

1. What is your favorite mystery series? Why is it your favorite?

2. What discovery have you made that you couldn't wait to share with someone else?

Searching the Scriptures

When the Bible refers to a mystery, it refers to something quite different from what we normally call a mystery. Paul explained a Biblical mystery in Ephesians 3:1–13 and unfolded other mysteries in other epistles.

In Ephesians 3:1 Paul introduced a prayer that he interrupted briefly but resumed in verse 14. He interrupted his prayer to discuss the mystery of the church, the Body of Christ.

Stewardship

In Ephesians 3:2–9 Paul explained the revelation of the mystery as a divine disclosure of a truth previously hidden. In verse 2 he mentioned the "dispensation of the grace of God." The word "dispensation" denotes "stewardship." A steward was responsible to his master for what he had entrusted to him. God had appointed Paul as His steward to present the truth that all believers share a unity in Christ. Paul saw himself as the steward "of the grace of God." He knew he did not deserve the privilege of declaring the mystery of unity in Christ. He recognized that God had graciously chosen him.

3. What stewardship has God entrusted to every believer? (See Matthew 28:18–20.)

4. What letter grade would you give to rate the church's fulfillment of this stewardship? Why?

Paul did not learn this mystery from another human being (Ephesians 3:3) or discover it on his own. He received the information by direct revelation from God.

5. How has God revealed Himself and His will to us?

Characteristics of a Mystery

A Biblical mystery always has three characteristics. First, it deals with something unknown. Paul alluded to this characteristic when he wrote, "Which in other ages was not made known unto the sons of men" (v. 5). Consequently, it is useless to search through the Old Testament to find passages that reveal a New Testament mystery.

Second, a Biblical mystery was revealed in the New Testament period. Paul wrote, "It is now revealed unto his holy apostles and prophets" (Ephesians 3:5; cf. Colossians 1:26).

Third, a Biblical mystery is disclosed only by divine revelation. Paul said the Holy Spirit had revealed the mystery to him (Ephesians 3:5).

The Mystery of the Church

The letter to the Ephesians deals primarily with the church, the Body of Christ, and the mystery of the church lies at the core of this teaching. The mystery affirms "that the Gentiles should be fellowheirs, and of the same body, and partakers of his promise in Christ by the gospel" (v. 6).

The Old Testament shows that God included Gentiles in the scope of His forgiveness. The book of Jonah makes this truth clear, but the Old Testament did not reveal the truth that the Gentiles would become one with the Jews in the Body of Christ—"fellowheirs, and of the same body" (v. 6).

During the New Testament period, God revealed to Paul and to others that the church would include Jews and Gentiles united in Christ.

6. On a practical level, what are a few implications of equality in Christ regardless of cultural backgrounds?

7. Do you agree or disagree that unbelievers see Christians setting a good example of harmony with those of different cultural backgrounds? Explain.

We do not find it hard to picture Jewish believers and Gentile believers united in one Body; after all, it has been that way for nearly two thousand years. But for the first-century believers, it was quite a revelation. Until then, Jews would not even eat with a Gentile. Before the apostle Peter would go to the Gentile Cornelius, God had to give him a revelation to prepare him (Acts 10:1–34). Peter needed to learn that God did not consider Gentiles "unclean." This revelation to Peter illustrates what Paul meant in Ephesians 3:5 when he claimed that God had revealed the mystery to His "holy apostles and prophets." God revealed truth about this mystery to others in addition to Paul.

Fellow Heirs, Members, and Partakers

Paul used three terms in verse 6 to describe the new relationship of believing Jews and believing Gentiles. The Gentiles had become fellow heirs, fellow members, and fellow partakers.

8. Read Ephesians 3:6. What does it mean to be a fellow heir?

For Jews and Gentiles, being fellow heirs means that Gentile believers have the same legal status as believing Jews. They receive the same blessings that Jewish believers receive as believers. (This truth does not mean Gentile believers may claim the promises God gave to Israel. For example, God promised Israel the land of Palestine, but the promise does not apply to Gentile believers.) Being fellow heirs does, however, mean that anything a believing Jew has in Christ, a believing Gentile has. All participate equally in the new life in Christ. All can share in the same peace that Christ gives. All have direct access to God the Father through Christ. The Bible teaches that we are heirs of God (Galatians 3:28, 29; 4:7) and joint heirs with Christ (Romans 8:16, 17).

Being fellow members indicates that both believing Jews and believing Gentiles are part of the Body of Christ, the church. Saved Gentiles share a position of equality with saved Jews in the church.

Jewish and Gentile believers are also fellow partakers of the promise. The word "promise" most likely refers to all spiritual blessings that the church possesses. This list of blessings includes regeneration, indwelling by the Holy Spirit, and many more gifts of God's grace.

The Minister of the Mystery

In Ephesians 3:7–9 Paul revealed more about himself as the minister of the mystery. He wrote about his character, his qualifications, and his task. First he claimed, "I was made a minister." The word "minister" means "servant." Before God saved Paul on the road to Damascus (see Acts 9), Paul was a proud, self-righteous Pharisee, but he became a new man in Christ.

9. Read Ephesians 3:7. Paul was made a minister according to what?

Paul's humility comes across clearly in his description of himself.

10. Read Ephesians 3:8. How did Paul describe himself?

11. Read Matthew 11:29. What qualities characterized both Jesus' and Paul's ministries?

12. What considerations should keep every believer humble as he or she serves God?

13. Why is humility a prerequisite to reaching out to unbelievers of

differing cultures and backgrounds?

Robert Morrison, who pioneered missions to China, informed his friends in England that he needed an assistant. Hearing of this need, a young man offered himself to the mission board, but initially the board decided he was too young, rough, and unpolished for missionary work. Later, however, the board told him, "We do not think you fit to be a missionary, but if you would like to go out as a servant to the missionary, we will send you."

The young man answered, "Well, if the gentlemen don't think me fit to be a missionary, I will go as a servant. I am willing to be a hewer of wood and a drawer of water or do anything to help the cause of my Heavenly Master."

That humble young man went out as a servant, but in time became a missionary. He was William Milne, one of the most outstanding missionaries to China.

Paul received a significant revelation from God about the church, but he did not let this privilege swell his head. He stayed humble. We, too, are privileged to know the way of salvation and the wonder of being united in Christ with believers everywhere, but humility should characterize us. True spiritual understanding includes knowing that we are what we are by the grace of God.

The Minister's Task

God never prepares a person to do a job unless He has a job for that person to do. Paul's task was twofold. First he was to "preach among the Gentiles the unsearchable riches of Christ."

14. Read Ephesians 3:8. What are some of the "unsearchable riches of Christ"?

Paul's task also included helping the Gentiles see that they had the same spiritual standing as the Jews (3:9). Although God revealed this truth to Paul in the first century, He had formulated it before creation (v. 9). The salvation of the Jews and Gentiles and their equal standing in the Body of Christ has always been in God's mind—and on His heart!

15. Does a church usually think of the riches of Christ as fully available to Muslims? Why or why not?

16. How might a typical church react to a sudden influx of Muslims into the neighborhood surrounding the church?

17. How would God expect the church to respond?

Purpose of the Mystery

Paul concluded his teachings on the mystery of Christ by citing the purpose of the mystery—to teach the holy angels about the manifold wisdom of God (v. 10). Angels are well-acquainted with God's power—particularly the power He showed in creation—but the many facets of God's wisdom are still unfolding for the angels. Watching God's church helps them understand God's wisdom in uniting Jews and Gentiles in one Body.

18. Read Ephesians 3:11. How do we know God's plan to create the church was not just a spur-of-the-moment decision?

As part of God's church, all believers can go to God with boldness and can, in essence, walk right into His presence (v. 12). This access is granted by God as a blessing of salvation. Judaism allowed access to the presence of God by the high priest only once a year on the Day of

Atonement. Bold access to God is a tremendous blessing for Jewish and Gentile believers alike! Opportunity for access to God is also a tremendous message to share.

19. Read Ephesians 3:13. What was Paul willing to endure so he could share the mystery of Christ with groups of people from widely different cultures and backgrounds?

Making It Personal

20. Which of the "unsearchable riches of Christ" do you appreciate the most? Why?

21. Name one of your neighbors who you think would like to have the riches in Christ that you enjoy.

22. Lay out a plan to communicate those riches to that neighbor.

23. Memorize Ephesians 3:8 and 9, and use these verses as a challenge to take the riches of Christ to unbelievers regardless of their culture or background.

Paul's Brief Big Prayer

Prayer is vital to spiritual growth.

Ephesians 3:14–21

"Now unto him that is able to do exceeding abundantly above all that we ask or think, according to the power that worketh in us, unto him be glory in the church by Christ Jesus throughout all ages, world without end. Amen" **(Ephesians 3:20, 21).**

Have you sung the words, "Sweet hour of prayer, sweet hour of prayer, that calls me from a world of care"? These words appear in "Sweet Hour of Prayer," a hymn with an international background. A Congregational minister named William Walford wrote the text in 1842 in England. Thomas Salmon carried Walford's poem to the United States, where it was published in *The New York Observer* in 1845. The first hymnal to include this text was the Baptist edition of *Church Melodies*. After the poem was printed in the hymnal, William Bradbury, a noted American gospel hymn composer and organist, gave the words its music. Soon people around the world were singing the song, and it has remained a favorite over the years.

In this lesson we will study the apostle Paul's prayer for the Ephesians. We will find that prayer is not only a sweet hour; it is also vital to spiritual growth.

Getting Started

1. What is your favorite song or Scripture verse that emphasizes prayer?

2. What makes prayer sweet for you?

Searching the Scriptures

Sometimes when someone talks with a friend, he or she begins to say something but suddenly changes the subject. After a while, though, the speaker returns to his or her original subject with, "As I was saying. . . ." In Ephesians 3:1 Paul started to pray, but he digressed to explain the mystery of the church. He did not resume his prayer until verse 14, in which he addressed God the Father.

3. Read Ephesians 3:14. What did Paul indicate about his heart by bowing his knees to God?

Part of the Family of God

Ephesians 3:15 is not teaching the universal fatherhood of God to all mankind. Scripture makes it clear that not all of mankind can claim God as their Father.

4. Read John 8:37–44. What was true of those Jews who claimed God was their Father even though they rejected Christ?

"Family" in Ephesians 3:15 refers to the saints of all the ages who have placed their trust in God. Only those who place their faith in God have the right to call Him Father. Being a son of the Father is a tremendous privilege. Paul was reinforcing the relationship that both the believing Jews and Gentiles in Ephesus enjoyed with God their Father.

5. What are some characteristics of an ideal father?

6. How do those characteristics carry over into the relationship a believer enjoys with his or her Heavenly Father?

7. How should praying to God as his or her Father affect a believer's prayers?

Strengthened with Might

In Ephesians 3:16 Paul began his prayer to the Heavenly Father. He prayed that God would grant his readers "to be strengthened with might by his Spirit in the inner man." The term "inner man" refers to our rational self, the part of us that is conscious of our existence. The Spirit that Paul referred to is the Holy Spirit, the strengthener of the inner man. Paul prayed that the Ephesian believers would have divine enabling for the inner man, the true self.

We need this inner strength to fight the spiritual battles that confront us every day. In our own strength we would utterly fail, but God is all-powerful, and He can enable us to triumph. In the original language this verse stresses power. Paul placed no human limit on what he requested, for he prayed that God would grant his request "according to the riches of his [God's] glory." God's glory is boundless, and so is the inner enabling He can give us.

8. Read Ephesians 3:16. Why didn't Paul pray for the Ephesians' outward man, or physical bodies?

9. On what do most prayer requests focus at a typical church prayer meeting?

10. What does Paul's request teach believers about what should be the primary focuses of their prayers?

Notice that Paul did not pray that life would be problem free for the Ephesians. Rather, he prayed for God's abundant enabling to help the Ephesians meet life's challenges and grow through them.

At Home in Our Hearts

Have you ever visited someone's home and felt that your host or hostess was just putting up with you but really preferred that you did not stay? If you have, contrast that visit with a get-together with a close family member who loves hosting you and who sincerely wants you to extend your visit. If you keep both of those experiences in mind, you will better understand Paul's second prayer request.

Paul prayed "that Christ may dwell in your hearts by faith" (v. 17). At first this request may seem strange, because we know that Paul was praying for believers. We also know that those who place their trust in Christ are saved and that Christ dwells in them. So why did Paul make such a request?

As you recall from the reminder above, a person may stay in someone's home without being made to feel at home. The Greek word for "dwell" in verse 17 means "to settle down and be at home." Though Christ lives in the heart of every believer, He can "feel at home" only in the hearts of those who love Him and truly appreciate His fellowship.

11. Read Ephesians 3:17. How does the believer's daily faith in God help God to feel at home in the believer's heart?

Rooted in Love

Before Paul made his next prayer request, he commented that the Ephesians were "rooted and grounded in love" (v. 17). The tense of the Greek verbs indicates that this rooting and grounding had already taken place. When a person trusts in Christ as Savior, the Holy Spirit plants him or her in the love of Christ (Romans 5:5). Consequently, the believer can grow in his or her knowledge of divine love.

12. How important is the ground in which a plant is rooted?

13. How should being rooted in love affect a person?

Comprehending Love

As his third request, Paul prayed that the Ephesian believers would "be able to comprehend with all saints what is the breadth, and length, and depth, and height" (Ephesians 3:18). "Comprehend" means "to appropriate." He prayed, therefore, that the Ephesians would lay hold of the full measure of Christ's love.

14. How does Paul's request in Ephesians 3:18 relate to Jesus' teachings in John 15:1–17?

15. How would you describe each dimension of Christ's love?

    a. It is so broad that

    b. It is so long that

    c. It is so deep that

    d. It is so high that

Paul's fourth request was quite similar to his third. He prayed that believers might "know the love of Christ, which passeth knowledge" (Ephesians 3:19). We can know that someone loves us because that person tells us so. We can also know someone loves us by what he or she does for us. We can never comprehend the full extent of Christ's love, but we can fully comprehend that He loves us. We learn from the Bible that He loves us, and we can know He loves us from observing what He does in our lives.

16. What makes Christ's love unique and unnatural when compared to the world's love?

The fact that Paul prayed that the Ephesians would know Christ's love shows believers that demonstrating the love of Christ doesn't come naturally. God's enabling is necessary for those who want the love of Christ to flow from their roots and bear fruit in their lives. God's enabling comes through prayer.

17. What will knowing and appropriating Christ's love say to a watching world? (See John 13:34 and 35.)

Finally Paul wanted his readers to "be filled with all the fulness of God" (Ephesians 3:19). When believers are strengthened by the Holy Spirit, walking in fellowship with Christ, and appropriating the knowledge of His love, they gradually experience "the fulness of God." They reflect God in every aspect of life and move closer every day to the high and noble goal of being like Christ.

18. What will happen to the believer who tries to be like Christ but doesn't enlist his or her Father's help through prayer?

Exceedingly Abundantly Above All

Paul closed his brief big prayer with an amazing statement about God's ability to answer prayer (v. 20). The words "exceeding abundantly" are a super superlative meaning "incapable of being exhausted." God's power cannot be depleted. "Ask" is in the middle voice and therefore means "to ask for something for oneself." "Think" means "consider." Therefore, God is able to do "exceedingly super-abundantly" above and beyond all that we can ask for ourselves or even consider in our thoughts! What a truth!

The power that Paul so superlatively described is the exact power that works in the believer to make him or her like Christ (v. 20).

19. What excuses might believers give for not growing in the Lord?

20. Why does Ephesians 3:20 render all of those excuses invalid?

Asking is the key to unlocking God's power that Paul described in verse 20. God's awesome power is freed through prayer. Bowing the knee with a humble, reverent heart before the Father as Paul did opens the floodgates to the riches of God's power. As God worked in the lives of the Ephesians, and Paul was confident He would, there would be cause for rejoicing and thanksgiving.

21. Read Ephesians 3:21. Who deserves the glory for the display of the power of God in the life of a believer?

Paul made it clear to the Ephesians that prayer is a vital part of spiritual growth. His message rings true for believers today too.

Making It Personal

Paul's prayer is a model for us today. Though nothing is gained from simply repeating the prayer, you can rest assured that praying through the passage from a sincere heart will yield spiritual growth in your life.

22. How often do you pray for your own spiritual growth?

23. Review Ephesians 3:16–19. Write a prayer to God asking Him for the same requests that Paul made on behalf of the Ephesians.

24. Use Ephesians 3:16–19 as a list of prayer requests for five other people. Pray for them by name every day next week.

25. Memorize Ephesians 3:20 and 21. Close each of your times in prayer with these verses in mind. Give God the glory for what He has done and will do in your life and in the lives of those you pray for.

Working Together to Maintain Unity

Spiritual gifts contribute to church unity and growth.

Ephesians 4:1–16

"Speaking the truth in love, may grow up into him in all things, which is the head, even Christ: from whom the whole body fitly joined and compacted by that which every joint supplieth, according to the effectual working in the measure of every part, maketh increase of the body unto the edifying of itself in love" (Ephesians 4:15, 16).

Pity the motorist whose body operates independent of his mind! He enters a 20 mph school zone and wants to obey the speed limit, but his right foot decides to press the pedal to the medal. Within seconds, his car is racing past the school at 70 mph. Finally, his right foot lets up, but as he tries to turn right at the next intersection, his left hand overpowers his right hand, and his car makes an illegal sudden left turn right in front of a police officer.

You can only imagine what might happen if your hands and feet failed to respond to signals from your brain on your next excursion. Thankfully a healthy human body functions well because all its parts work harmoniously.

Getting Started

1. When have you felt like your brain and body were not connecting?

2. When have you felt like you weren't connecting with someone in your local church body?

Searching the Scriptures

In Ephesians 4:1–16 the apostle Paul underscored the importance of maintaining unity in the church, the Body of Christ. Referring to himself as "the prisoner of the Lord" (v. 1), he urged his readers to walk worthy of the vocation wherewith they were called. If they heeded this admonition, they would function as a unified church.

Although we must never compromise doctrine for the sake of unity, we must never let personal preferences disrupt our unity. Some things simply aren't worth fighting about.

3. What are some areas of personal preferences that could endanger church unity?

4. What does it say about a person's character if he or she insists, "It's either my way or the highway"?

Lowliness

In Ephesians 4:2 Paul named some attitudes that help build unity. He began with "lowliness," which is the opposite of arrogance and conceit. The ancient pagans despised this virtue, but Jesus elevated it to a place of high value. He ministered humbly, giving Himself without measure for others. The Cross demonstrated His humility in an unprecedented manner.

5. What does the world say about where lowliness will get you in life?

6. Why is lowliness essential in members of a church?

Paul also named meekness as an attitude that helps build unity. At first we may think meekness is weakness, but it is the opposite. Meekness demands inner strength, because it is gentleness in action. It refuses to lash out at those who provoke or persecute us. When Jesus was reviled, He refused to respond vindictively. Instead He submitted to the Father's will; and, as a lamb led to the slaughter (Isaiah 53:7), He offered Himself on the cross as the perfect sacrifice for our offenses (1 Peter 2:18–24).

If we show lowliness and meekness, we will not throw a temper tantrum when the congregation decides to install carpet instead of tile. We will not threaten to split the church when the pastor preaches overtime four Sundays in a row or doesn't preach in the particular style we like. Nor will we feel insulted when asked to sign up for nursery duty. We will not consider ourselves too big for any "small" ministry.

7. What "small" ministries often lack workers in many churches?

8. Read John 13:13–15. What service did Jesus perform that the disciples must have thought was beneath them?

Long-suffering

Paul also encouraged the Ephesians to be long-suffering (Ephesians 4:2). This word carries the idea of patient endurance even under persistent provocation. Long-suffering Christians do not give up on fellow believers who consistently fail the Lord in certain areas. They endeavor to help their Christian brothers and sisters grow in Christ.

Further, long-suffering Christians do not abandon the local church when the going gets tough. If attendance falls, they remain faithful in attendance. If the missions fund slumps, they increase their giving.

Forbearance

Paul exhorted the Ephesians to forbear one another (v. 2). To forbear means to control yourself when someone provokes you. It also means to be patient and to show self-restraint. Not everyone does things the way we do. We need to make allowances for their diversity, their failures and faults, their background and training (or lack of it), their abilities (or lack of them), and their temperaments.

9. Read Ephesians 4:2. With what attitude does forbearance need to be carried out?

10. Why is the statement "I don't like him" or "I don't like her" not a valid reason to refrain from showing forbearance?

11. As you think about the personalities of Jesus' disciples, which disciples do you think were the hardest to get along with? Why?

Christ called His disciples to God's service with their personalities in mind. In a similar manner, God places people in churches with their personalities in mind. To refuse to forebear with the people in your church is to say to God that you could do a better job at bringing just the right people to your church.

12. How does having a variety of personalities in the local church benefit its ministry?

Endeavoring to Keep Unity

Finally Paul pleaded with the Ephesians to attempt "to keep the unity of the Spirit in the bond of peace" (v. 3). Some Christians think that if we believers endure wrong without openly striking back, we have done our Christian duty. However, Paul's teaching went far beyond such a concept.

13. Read Ephesians 4:3. What does the word "endeavouring" suggest about the task of keeping unity in a local church?

14. What are some ways a church can endeavor to keep unity?

Shared Oneness

In Ephesians 4:4–6 Paul identified a sevenfold oneness that believers share. This oneness is the basis for building true Christian unity.

First, this oneness includes "one body" (v. 4). The Body is the church. God did not intend one church for Jewish believers and another for Gentile believers. Both belong to the same church. All believers, regardless of culture or national origin, are members of the Body of Christ.

Second, the oneness involves "one Spirit," the Holy Spirit (v. 4). The Spirit Who fell upon the Jews at Pentecost (see Acts 2) also fell upon the Gentiles at the home of Cornelius (see Acts 10). We may have different preferences and temperaments, but we share the same indwelling Holy Spirit (Romans 8:9).

Third, believers share "one hope" (Ephesians 4:4). We share the hope of spending eternity in Heaven with Christ and participating in His glory (Titus 1:2).

Fourth, the oneness means that all believers share "one Lord," the Lord Jesus Christ (Ephesians 4:5). Since all true believers serve the same Lord, we should seek to serve Him together in our local churches.

Fifth, the oneness involves "one faith" (v. 5). God saves all believers in the same way: each one must place his or her faith in Jesus Christ (Romans 10:9–17). You cannot be a true Christian without having trusted in Christ (Acts 4:10–12). The world believes many roads lead to God, but Jesus proclaimed, "I am the way, the truth, and the life: no man cometh unto the Father, but by me" (John 14:6).

Sixth, believers have "one baptism" in common (Ephesians 4:5). Paul was not referring to water baptism in this verse. He was referring to Spirit baptism, which places us into the Body of Christ. First Corinthians 12:13 declares, "For by one Spirit are we all baptized into one body."

Seventh, the oneness includes "one God and Father" (Ephesians 4:6). Mankind has worshiped many idols and false gods, but only one true God exists (Deuteronomy 4:39; Psalms 95:3; 135:5).

15. Read Ephesians 4:4–6. Which truths in these verses do you believe give a local church the most assurance that unity is possible?

Spiritual Gifts

Although God has placed all believers into the same Body, He has given each one particular spiritual gifts (Ephesians 4:7). When we exercise our gifts properly, they strengthen the unity that exists among members of the church.

Like a conquering hero returning home, Jesus Christ ascended to Heaven after defeating sin, death, and Satan at Calvary. Once Home, He gave His subjects gifts with which to serve Him (vv. 8–10).

In Ephesians 4:11 the apostle Paul listed a few spiritual gifts. In Romans 12 and 1 Corinthians 12 he listed other spiritual gifts. He began his list in Ephesians 4 with the gift of apostle. God provided the apostles for founding the church. Now that the church's foundation has been

built, the Spirit does not give the gift of apostleship to anyone
today.

The New Testament church also had the gift of prophets (Ephesians
4:11). They declared God's will to the church until the Bible was fully
written. Today the Bible is complete, so the Holy Spirit no longer gives
the gift of prophets.

Third, Paul listed evangelists (v. 11). Today when we think of an
evangelist, we picture a traveling preacher inviting sinners to come to
Christ for salvation. In terms of the New Testament, however, this gift
referred more to traveling missionaries, who won people to Christ and
then established new local churches.

Fourth, Paul mentioned "pastors and teachers" (v. 11). These two
words probably refer to two aspects of the same office. The word "pastor" indicates a shepherd. This gifted person cares for a flock, a local
body of believers, and feeds them by teaching them the Word of God.

Using Spiritual Gifts

16. Read Ephesians 4:12. What is the responsibility of the pastor?

17. What are the responsibilities of the church members?

18. Read Ephesians 4:13–16. If believers are faithful in fulfilling their
ministries in a local church, what will be the results?

As believers in a church continue to mature, they will deepen in
their love for one another.

19. Read Ephesians 4:15. How is "speaking the truth in love" a sign
of unity and maturity among believers?

20. Read Ephesians 4:16. By implication, what happens when believers refuse to be equipped for service and take part in the edification of other believers?

Making It Personal

21. What have you done to endeavor to keep the unity of your local church?

22. With what fellow church members do you need to seek restoration? Plan to do it as soon as possible.

23. In what areas of service are you currently involved at your church?

24. To what new areas of service might your spiritual gifts apply? Consider investigating those new areas and asking your church leaders for guidance and any necessary equipping.

25. Memorize Ephesians 4:15 and 16. Write a prayer of commitment to God to do your part in your local church to build unity by serving Him.

Lesson 9

Walk This Way

God expects believers to live according to the new man.

Ephesians 4:17–32

"That ye put off concerning the former conversation the old man, which is corrupt according to the deceitful lusts; and be renewed in the spirit of your mind; and that ye put on the new man, which after God is created in righteousness and true holiness" (Ephesians 4:22–24).

Excitement rippled through the air on January 19, 1977, in Allahabad, Uttar Pradesh, India, at the spot where the Yamuna River flows into the Ganges. More than 12.7 million Hindus had gathered for the festival of Kumbh Mela. The event set a record as the biggest gathering of people for a single purpose in history.

For the Hindus it was the holiest day in nearly 150 years, because that morning the planets aligned for a brief time. The alignment began at 9:28 and ended twelve minutes later at 9:40. The Hindus considered those twelve minutes the holiest time of the holiest day. During that brief period only 200,000 of the 12.7 million Hindu pilgrims immersed themselves in the Ganges, believing the Ganges would wash away the sins of a lifetime.

We cannot fault the Hindus' desire for cleansing from sin, but we can fault the way they tried to receive the cleansing. Only the blood of Jesus offers a new and changed life.

73

In Ephesians 4:17–32 Paul clearly laid out the truths that teach us how to change and become more like Christ.

Getting Started

1. What are some ways people try to better themselves?

2. What are the true results of their efforts?

Searching the Scriptures

The Way Unbelievers Walk

Paul urged the Ephesians to no longer live like their unsaved peers. He instructed them to "walk not as other Gentiles walk" (Ephesians 4:17). Our lives should clearly differ from those of the unsaved. The unsaved behave differently because they think differently. Their minds are "vanity," or aimless, Paul wrote (v. 17). They are like stray sheep. Unaware of their lost condition, they wander away from the only One Who can rescue them.

3. What goals do unbelievers set for themselves to gain a sense of purpose in life?

4. What evidence have you seen that unbelievers know they are headed nowhere in life?

Unbelievers' understanding is darkened (v. 18). They live in a world of illusion. They are blind to spiritual truth because they have rejected the knowledge of God (cf. Romans 1:21; 1 Corinthians 2:14).

Moreover, they are alienated from "the life of God" (Ephesians 4:18). Sweet fellowship comes from a close walk with the Lord. The unsaved know nothing of this fellowship. They live far from God.

The word "blindness" at the end of verse 18 could be rendered "hardness." The unsaved have hardened their hearts against God. They are insensitive to the Lord and to sin. They have ignored the pain of a guilty conscience and now are callous toward God. According to verse 19, the Gentiles had given themselves over to lewdness.

5. Read Ephesians 4:19. What drives the unbeliever whose conscience has been silenced by his or her repeatedly sinning?

Christians should be different from unbelievers. Believers should repudiate evil because they have "learned," or have a vital relationship with, Christ (v. 20). Knowing Christ gives believers the opportunity to keep greediness from controlling their lives.

6. What replaces greediness in the life of the believer who is closely connected with Christ? (See Ephesians 3:17–19).

Off with the Old

In Ephesians 4:22–24 Paul commanded believers to put off the old way of life and put on the new. We should put off the rags of the attitudes and actions associated with the old life and display the robes of righteousness God gave us when He saved us (Ephesians 4:22; 2 Corinthians 5:21). The "old man" grows corrupt and has no claim of dominance in the believer's life. The old man has lost the war but still desires to control the believer's attitudes and actions.

7. Read Ephesians 4:22. What deceitful promises excite the lusts of the "old man"?

A New Mind

Putting off the old man happens as a believer's mind is renewed (v. 23; Romans 12:1, 2). Day by day the believer is changed to be more like Christ. The believer lays aside the garments of the old man and no longer believes the deceitful promises that excite the lusts of the old man.

8. Read John 17:17. What did Jesus pray concerning His disciples?

Appropriating the Word of God by faith causes spiritual growth. As believers grow, they don the "new man" garments instead of the old. Their attitudes and actions more frequently resemble Christ's. They are sanctified, or set apart, for God's use.

9. Read Ephesians 4:24. After Whom is the new man patterned?

10. Contrast the description of the new man in verse 24 with the description of the lifestyle of the old man in verses 17–19.

The Ephesian believers who were living according to the old man must have been touched deeply by the truths in chapter 4. The Holy Spirit recorded the truths so they and we might know that indeed "the truth is in Jesus" (v. 21) and that we might all live by faith as God intended us to live (v. 24).

So what does living by the new man look like? Starting with verse 25, Paul offered practical applications of what it means to have the new man at the controls of a believer's life.

Speaking Honestly

Paul began by exhorting the Ephesians to put away lying (v. 25). Deceitfulness defiles a Christian. Speaking the truth is a Biblical principle found not only in Ephesians 4 but also in Zechariah 8:16, which

Paul quoted when he added, "Speak every man truth with his neigh-
bour" (Ephesians 4:25).

11. Read Ephesians 4:25. "Members one of another" refers to fellow
church members. What lies do church members tell one another?

12. Why is honesty between believers so important? (See Ephesians
4:15.)

Righteous Anger

Ephesians 4:26 may surprise you. You might expect to read, "Do not
become angry!" But you read, "Be ye angry." Before we jump to con-
clusions, we need to know that anger is an emotion and in itself is not
wrong. What makes anger right or wrong is what a person does with
it. Anger becomes sinful when it is used for selfish reasons, is used to
attack people instead of problems, or is allowed to fester. For example,
if Jason's teacher calls Jason's dad and tells him that his son was caught
in a lie at school, the dad will most likely experience anger. If the father
uses his anger's energy to scream and holler at his son, then he has
sinned in his anger. However, if the father uses his anger's energy to
lovingly help his son deal with the sin, then his anger would not be sinful. Anger used for God's glory is not sinful anger.

13. Read Matthew 21:12 and 13. What made Jesus angry? How did
He respond?

14. What would life be like if we could not feel anger?

The Bible forbids sinful anger. After Paul instructed, "Be ye angry," he added, "and sin not: let not the sun go down upon your wrath." By refusing to take care of our sinful anger immediately, we give the Devil a foothold in our lives (Ephesians 4:26, 27).

15. Read Ephesians 4:27. Why does letting sinful anger fester give the Devil a foothold in a believer's life?

Working Hard

"Let him that stole steal no more," Paul wrote in verse 28. His exhortation can be rendered, "Let him that is stealing steal no more."

We don't have to be armed robbers to steal. We may steal from our employers by wasting time or spending it on something other than our job responsibilities. Supervisors may steal credit for the ideas or work their employees produced. Some believers cheat on their income tax returns.

16. How else could a believer be guilty of stealing?

Paul exhorted his readers at Ephesus to, instead of stealing, work faithfully (v. 28).

17. Read Ephesians 4:28. What reason did Paul give for working?

Clean Speech

In verse 29 Paul commanded his readers not to let any "corrupt communication" come out of their mouths. The word "corrupt" indicates "rotten" or "decayed," but it also means "worthless" or "useless." We should avoid foul language, dirty stories, and off-color jokes. We should also refrain from idle words (Matthew 12:36).

It is not enough to rid our lives of these "corrupt" forms of communication, however. We must replace them with something beneficial.

18. Read Ephesians 4:29. What should a believer's words do for other people?

Avoiding Grief

Sin in the believer's life grieves the Spirit (Ephesians 4:30). For this reason, we must always watch how we live. We must always guard against sin.

The Holy Spirit dwelling in us acts as God's seal that we are His. This seal will stay with us until the day God redeems our mortal bodies and gives us our new, glorified bodies (v. 30). The Spirit's presence should remind us that we cannot get away with living in sin. His presence should also encourage us, since He is always ready to help us overcome our sin.

In the closing two verses of Ephesians 4, Paul gave further exhortations concerning godly living.

19. Read Ephesians 4:31 and 32. What is the basis for showing kindness, compassion, and forgiveness to a fellow believer?

Making It Personal

The Christian's walk should differ dramatically from that of the unbeliever. The Christian's interests, pleasures, desires, and goals are supposed to align with God's will. The unbeliever, on the other hand, lives to fulfill selfish lusts and attain selfish goals. However, the word "walk" suggests progression. No Christian has arrived spiritually. Each of us Christians should be making progress in our fellowship with Christ and in our resemblance to Him. Why not take some big steps forward this week?

20. In what areas of your life have you repeatedly trusted deceitful promises that excite your flesh?

☐ Your language?

☐ Your attitudes?

☐ Your ambitions?

☐ Your relationships?

☐ Your habits?

☐ Your leisure activities?

☐ Your work?

21. Confess to God any sinful trust in deceitful promises that you recognized in your life.

22. Identify those whom you may have wronged by your sin and seek forgiveness from them.

23. Endeavor to immerse your mind in the true Word of God. What verses or passages will you meditate on this week?

24. Memorize Ephesians 4:22–24. Post this passage in places where you spend time doing tasks that take little thought (e.g., dashboard of your car, bathroom mirror, bedroom nightstand). Use the verses as a reminder of your need to renew your mind on a daily basis.

Love and Light

A believer's love shows light to a dark world.

Ephesians 5:1–17

"And walk in love, as Christ also hath loved us, and hath given himself for us an offering and a sacrifice to God for a sweetsmelling savour. . . . For ye were sometimes darkness, but now are ye light in the Lord: walk as children of light" (Ephesians 5:2, 8).

Love and light have no obvious connections. Love comes from within us, while light comes from outside us. Love is felt, while light is seen. Love can be reciprocated, while light can only be reflected. Yet Paul brought the qualities of love and light together in a unique way and demonstrated a vital connection between the two.

Getting Started

1. What are some qualities of love and light?

2. How might love and light form a vital connection?

Imitating God

Paul exhorted believers to be "followers of God, as dear children" (Ephesians 5:1). This exhortation suggests we imitate God. Just as a son or daughter usually takes on some of the characteristics and mannerisms of a parent, so Christians should resemble their Heavenly Father's moral characteristics and godly ways. "Dear children" can be rendered "children of love." God is love. As His children, we, too, should be loving individuals.

Love, the greatest of all virtues (1 Corinthians 13:13), is seen most clearly in Christ, Who came to earth to show us the Father (John 1:18; 14:8, 9). Our Savior loves us so much that He died on the cross for us. His sacrificial death was "an offering and a sacrifice to God as a sweet-smelling savour" (Ephesians 5:2).

The Old Testament used the term "sweetsmelling savour" to describe the smoke of an offering as it rose heavenward to God. The term also pictures God accepting that offering and finding it pleasant. When Christ offered Himself for our sins, He won God's full approval. The Father accepted His sacrifice.

3. Read Ephesians 5:2 and Leviticus 1:1–9. Compare and contrast the burnt offering of the Old Testament with Christ's sacrifice.

Guarding against Immorality

In Ephesians 5:3–8 Paul urged his readers to guard their lives against the works of darkness. The apostle John concurred, noting that "God is light, and in him is no darkness at all" (1 John 1:5). Darkness represents sin; and light, holiness. Because we belong to God's family and imitate our Father, we should not walk in darkness. Paul warned believers against a number of evils associated with darkness. They fall into three categories: immorality, covetousness, and sins associated with speech.

In Ephesians 5:3 Paul warned against immorality. Our word "pornography" comes from the Greek word translated "fornication" in verse 3. It refers to every kind of illicit sex. In our day, accounts of illicit sex bombard us on every hand. The sexual revolution changed Western society. Paul's warning is as relevant today as it was in his day.

Paul continued in his warning against immorality by listing "uncleanness" (v. 3). Moral uncleanness includes reading filthy literature, looking at obscene photographs or videos, and doing any other indecent activities.

4. How concerned is the immoral person with the needs of others? Explain.

Guarding against Covetousness

Covetousness is a desire for more and more. Paul warned the Ephesian believers against such desires (v. 3).

5. How concerned is the covetous person with the needs of others?

Paul warned the Ephesians, "Let it [fornication, uncleanness, and covetousness] not be once named among you, as becometh saints" (v. 3). In other words, the Ephesian believers should have had no reason to even talk about such sins, because the sins were not to be part of their lives. Saints are to be set apart for God's use. Believers who mix sin into their lives are hampering God's ability to use them.

Guarding Your Tongue

Paul also warned against sins of the tongue (v. 4). He explained that filthiness has no part in a believer's life. Filthiness may take the form of coarse, obscene, vulgar talk. We should not read, listen to, or tell dirty stories or suggestive jokes.

Paul mentioned "foolish talking" as the next sin of the tongue (v. 4). This term refers to empty, silly, worthless talk. Jesting, which he also forbade, connotes joking about sin. Paul neither implied nor commanded us not to have a sense of humor or to enjoy a good, clean joke. We can display a sense of humor, but we must recognize that sin is no laughing matter. These sins of speech that Paul named are not fitting or proper for believers.

6. Read Ephesians 5:4. How do Paul's instructions relate to watching movies and television shows that contain vulgar language?

7. What does believers' enthusiastically talking about movies and TV programs that contain vulgar language communicate to unbelievers around them?

Instead of using our tongues in sinful ways, we should use them to give God thanks (v. 4). We should celebrate the Lord's goodness every day, not just on an annual holiday, as a day of thanksgiving.

8. What does our being thankful even when times are tough tell others about our God?

In Ephesians 5:5 Paul asserted that no fornicator, unclean person, or covetous person has any part in God's kingdom. This verse warns against the serious and eternal consequences of living apart from God. But does it teach that those who have committed these sins can never be saved? Obviously not, because in his letter to the Corinthian Christians, Paul mentioned that some of them had been saved from such a lifestyle (1 Corinthians 6:9–11). Whoever genuinely believes on Christ for salvation receives forgiveness and a new life regardless of his or her former lifestyle. Yet all believers are capable of committing the sins that Paul listed.

Be Not Deceived

Many who practice immorality and other vices try to make their sins appear innocent so others will be more apt to join them in their sins. They do this so they can ease their own consciences. Such people are deceivers.

9. Read Ephesians 5:6. What truth did Paul state to counteract the deceivers?

In verse 7 Paul made a connection between the coming wrath of God on unbelievers (v. 6) and believers' lives.

10. Read Ephesians 5:7. Why should knowing that the wrath of God is coming for unbelievers motivate us to be different from them?

Walking in the Light

Choosing to be like the world is the most unloving thing a believer could do to unbelievers, because believers who choose to follow the world are choosing to extinguish the light of the gospel that God desires to shine in their lives. "Walk as children of light" is God's plan for believers (v. 8). Walking as children of light will result in a life characterized by goodness, righteousness, and truth (v. 9)—virtues that are much different from unbelievers' characteristics.

Goodness forbids a believer from doing anything that would harm others. We should not seek our own pleasure or profit at the expense of someone else. When righteousness characterizes a believer, he or she has integrity in all dealings. And when truth characterizes the believer, he or she is honest and realistic in all areas, not just in speech.

11. Compare the trio of virtues in verse 9 with the trios of sins in verses 3 and 4.

12. Read Ephesians 5:9. Who makes it possible to live like a "verse 9 Christian" instead of a "verses 3 and 4 Christian"?

Ephesians 5:10 continues the thought of verse 8; we are to walk as children of light, "proving what is acceptable unto the Lord." We are to test all our thoughts, words, and deeds by the standard of God's Word and to approve the things that stand the test. When we consider taking a certain action, we should decide according to whether or not the Lord finds it acceptable, not according to who else is doing it.

Exposing Sin

Just as verse 9 lists the fruit of light, verse 11 clarifies the fruitlessness of darkness. We believers must not participate with others in the works of darkness. But beyond that, we should reprove, or expose them. The word "reprove" indicates that we should put them under conviction. Exposing sin in the life of an unbeliever is in reality a loving thing to do. If an unbeliever doesn't know he or she is a sinner, then that person will never see the need for a Savior.

13. Read Ephesians 5:12 and 13. How can a believer effectively expose the darkness of an unbeliever?

According to Paul, anything that makes something else visible is light (v. 13). Believers are light in that sense. The light of Christ shining through us can cause unbelievers to see themselves in light of God's holiness and help them realize that they need to trust Christ as their Savior.

Have you ever been sound asleep and suddenly been awakened by someone shouting, "Wake up!"? Such a shout could jar a person to his senses in a hurry. In verse 14 Paul shouted, "Wake up!" to those in sin. "Arise from the dead," he counseled, "and Christ shall give thee light." Believers who live as if they are still dead in their sins won't shine for Christ.

Buying Up Opportunities

Paul reminded us that time is short and that we ought to make every moment count for the Lord. In Ephesians 5:15 he commanded, "See then that ye walk circumspectly." The word "circumspectly" means "carefully, cautiously, prudently."

14. Read Ephesians 5:15. Describe the differences between a fool and a wise person. (See Proverbs 12:15.)

Paul urged us to redeem the time (Ephesians 5:16). In the original language, the word for time refers to a critical period of time, or a special opportunity. "Redeem" literally means "to buy up." In other words, we are to buy up every opportunity, to "seize the moment" for the Lord.

15. Read Ephesians 5:16. Paul described the times in which he was living as "evil." What word would you use to describe the times in which we live?

16. Why should the decaying of society around us cause us to use our time wisely?

God gives us opportunities to obey Him each day. But to buy up these opportunities, we must know His will (v. 17).

17. Read Ephesians 5:1 and 2 and Matthew 5:13–16 and 22:37–39. What is God's will according to these passages?

We love God by loving others. Loving others demonstrates God's love to them. God's love is at the heart of the gospel message. When we show God's love through our lives, we become a beacon to unbelievers, who are all traveling through the darkness toward a tragic collision with God's wrath.

Making It Personal

18. How aware have you been of the connection between the love you show and the light you shine?

19. Who in your life desperately needs to see the light of the gospel?

20. How will you love that person this week as a demonstration of God's love for him or her?

21. Commit to pray that your life would be a consistent stream of love toward that person and that he or she would see the light of the gospel in both your words and deeds.

22. Memorize Ephesians 5:2 and 8. Write a motto to help you remember the truth of these verses (e.g., my love is my light).

Lesson 11

Spirit-controlled Relationships

Spirit-controlled believers build loving relationships.

Ephesians 5:18–33

"And be not drunk with wine, wherein is excess; but be filled with the Spirit. . . . Submitting yourselves one to another in the fear of God" (Ephesians 5:18, 21).

Though born into a Methodist family and raised a Methodist, Philip P. Bliss became a Baptist at the age of twelve, when he joined the Baptist church of Cherry Flats, Pennsylvania. His godly parents had prayer and Bible study at family devotions; they also spent considerable time in family singing.

Bliss became one of the most prolific gospel songwriters of his time. He wrote the music for such songs as "I Gave My Life for Thee" and "It Is Well with My Soul." He often composed the music for many of his own words.

But Bliss was more than a songwriter; he was also a family man. He loved his wife dearly. He proved this love on December 29, 1876, at the age of thirty-eight. He and his wife had taken a train that passed through Ohio. When the train crossed a bridge near Ashtabula, Ohio, the bridge collapsed, and the train cars fell many feet into the river below.

Bliss freed himself from the wreckage, but the train caught fire with his wife trapped inside. In spite of the fire, Bliss went back into the burning car to rescue his wife. He willingly risked his life to save hers. His attempt failed, however, and they both perished in the flames.

Philip P. Bliss is an example not only of a man whose life counted for God, but also of a man whose love for his wife knew no bounds.

In Ephesians 5:18–33 Paul addressed the type of love and submission it takes to build strong relationships—especially a marriage.

Getting Started

1. What does the world think it takes to make a relationship work?

2. Some would say that a great marriage is not only hard but impossible. Would you agree or disagree with that statement? Why?

Searching the Scriptures

Controlled by the Spirit

Paul wrote about Christian families, not about families in general. Before he began to discuss the subject, he discussed an important truth that is foundational to a successful marriage. The concept Paul taught involves being controlled continuously by the Spirit. It is impossible to have a successful Christian marriage unless the Spirit of God controls the relationship. His control is also essential to building a strong family unit and any other interpersonal relationship.

To help his readers understand what it means to be controlled by the Spirit, Paul gave a negative command that served to illustrate the idea.

3. Read Ephesians 5:18. What has alcohol done to people who are drunk? What parts of their lives does the alcohol seem to control?

When we let the Spirit control our lives, He changes us. We don't swagger around like someone who is drunk, but our lives are different. He gives us new desires. He changes our motives. He helps us turn our love for ourselves toward Him and others.

4. Read Romans 5:5. How does a Christian acquire the kind of love that honors the Lord?

5. Read 1 Corinthians 13:4–7. What characteristics of a Spirit-controlled love would be particularly helpful in a marriage?

Do not confuse the indwelling of the Spirit with the filling with the Spirit. Indwelling occurs at the moment of salvation. At that point the Holy Spirit comes to live permanently in the believer. We will never get more of Him or have less of Him indwelling us. The filling of the Spirit does not involve our getting more of the Spirit but rather with His getting more of us. He wants to control our minds, our hearts, and our actions. Filling equals control. When we are filled with the Spirit, the Spirit controls us.

The Spirit Gives Joy

A characteristic of being controlled by the Spirit is the desire to praise the Lord. Spirit-controlled Christians have joy and express this joy in "psalms and hymns and spiritual songs" (Ephesians 5:19). Consider Paul and Silas: although unjustly beaten and thrown into prison in Philippi, they sang praises to God (Acts 16:22–25).

6. Read Ephesians 5:19. What about the Lord should cause a Spirit-controlled person to sing?

7. How would a relationship, especially a marital relationship, be affected if both people were filled with joy and had a song to the Lord in their hearts?

The Spirit Makes Us Thankful

Spirit-controlled Christians also express gratitude. They give "thanks always for all things" (Ephesians 5:20).

8. What "all things" in a marriage are sometimes hard to be thankful for (e.g., dirty socks on the floor, burned grilled cheese again, snoring)?

9. What does having thankful spirits do to a relationship?

The Spirit Helps Us Submit

Another evidence of being under the Spirit's control is found in verse 21. Spirit-filled Christians submit to one another. Such an attitude does not come naturally; our old nature bristles at the very mention of submission. We want to be first, and we want to have the final say. We want to make the decisions. But if we are Spirit-controlled, we will put others' interests ahead of our own. This doesn't mean that a person in authority has to give up his or her position in order to submit to someone under him or her. But it does mean that a person in authority will use his or her position to *benefit* those under him or her.

10. Read John 13:3–17. How did Christ submit to His disciples? Did He lose any of His authority by submitting to them?

11. Read Ephesians 5:21. What is significant about submitting to one another "in the fear of God?" (See 1 Peter 5:5 and 6.)

In Ephesians 5:22 Paul continued to address relationships. But he focused specifically on roles in marriage.

The Spirit-controlled Wife

First Paul addressed wives. He wrote, "Wives, submit yourselves unto your own husbands, as unto the Lord" (v. 22). This exhortation runs contrary to the me-first philosophy prevalent in our culture, but a Christian wife should cooperate with the Lord's will for the husband-wife relationship. When she submits to her husband, she yields "as unto the Lord."

12. Read Ephesians 5:22. What makes it difficult for a wife to submit to her husband?

13. Why does submitting to Christ first make submitting to her husband attainable for a wife?

Women are certainly not inferior to men, and in some marriages, the wife is better educated and more talented than her husband. Furthermore, Christian married couples are coequal in Christ. However, their divinely appointed family roles are different.

The Spirit-controlled Husband

Although God appointed the husband to serve as the head of the home, he should not assume the role of a dictator. Paul commanded the husband to love his wife. If he loves her as he loves himself (Ephesians 5:25, 28; Colossians 3:19), he will lead by following the Lord. He will set the example in spiritual pursuits, and he will consider her desires, interests, and needs extremely important. The husband and wife will make plans together in submission to the Lord's will.

14. Read Ephesians 5:23. How did Paul underscore the deep love a husband is to have for his wife?

In verse 24 Paul again reinforced his point about wives submitting to their husbands by drawing a parallel between the husband-wife relationship and that of Christ and the church. Christ is the head of the church, and the church is subject to Him.

A wife finds it easier to submit to a husband who shows her love. And a husband finds it easier to love a wife who is submissive. Both responsibilities—love and submission—must be accepted for a Christian marriage to work well.

Christ's Love as the Example

Paul also set a high standard for husbands. He instructed them, "Husbands, love your wives, even as Christ also loved the church, and gave himself for it" (v. 25). Even unsaved husbands can love their wives, but Paul wrote about a love far beyond mere human love. A godly husband's love should know no bounds.

15. Read Ephesians 5:26 and 27. Christ's purpose in loving the church was to sanctify it and help it to grow. What can a husband do to lovingly help his wife grow spiritually?

Paul asserted, "So ought men to love their wives as their own bodies" (v. 28). When a man and a woman marry, they become one flesh (v. 31). We find this Biblical truth initially in Genesis 2:21–24, and Christ affirmed it in Mark 10:8. In Ephesians 5:33 Paul repeated his command to husbands: "Let every one of you in particular so love his wife even as himself."

Hold that thought for a moment. "As himself" means a husband will be as concerned about his wife's needs and desires as he is about his own. Every man is normally concerned about nourishing and caring for his own body (v. 29). Paul instructed husbands to take their strong desire to care for themselves and use it in caring for their wives.

16. What will happen to any selfish desires a husband has as he begins to reach out to his wife to meet her needs?

17. Read Ephesians 5:29. How does the Lord nourish and cherish the church?

18. How do Christ's actions on behalf of the church relate to how a husband should nourish and cherish his wife?

Leaving Mom and Dad

Still quoting Genesis 2:24, Paul explained in Ephesians 5:31, "For this cause shall a man leave his father and mother." When your children marry, leave them alone. Be available to give advice if they ask for it, but don't try to run their lives. The Bible instructs them to leave you, their parents, to start a new family unit, just as you did when you got married. If you encourage them to come running home every time they have a problem, you hinder them from establishing a strong bond of love and mutual respect.

19. How does deeply depending on one's parents hurt a person's relationship with his or her spouse?

20. After studying verses 22–33, why do you think it's important to keep verse 18 in mind?

Making It Personal

21. Review Ephesians 5:18–21.

a. How much joy have you had lately?

b. How often have you said thank you to God recently?

c. How have you submitted to the people around you?

22. Based on your answers to the questions in 21, evaluate how much control you have given the Spirit in your life. Summarize.

23. If you are married, plan three ways to submit to your spouse this week. Record your plan below.

24. Memorize Ephesians 5:18 and 21. Review these verses every morning. Submit to the control of the Spirit every day.

At Home and at Work

*God gives instructions for family
and work relationships.*

Ephesians 6:1–9

**"And, ye fathers, provoke not your children to
wrath: but bring them up in the nurture and
admonition of the Lord. Servants, be obedient
to them that are your masters according to the
flesh, with fear and trembling, in singleness of
your heart, as unto Christ" (Ephesians 6:4, 5).**

The family is under attack from secular forces. Even the definition of "family" depends on who uses the word. Most of us think a family consists of a mother, a father, and children, but we acknowledge that a family can consist of just one parent. Death or divorce can deprive children of one of their parents. There are also cases in which children lose both of their parents and live with another couple who assume the Biblical roles of mom and dad.

Many secularists perceive a family as any number of people living together in a bonded relationship. The relationship may involve two male adults or two female adults or an unmarried man and woman or— the possibilities seem endless.

God's original plan is to have one man and one woman become a family through marriage. They then have the opportunity to add children to their family through either birth or adoption. No amount of deviant practice and propaganda will ever change God's original plan for the family.

In his letter to the Ephesians, Paul gave instructions to families. He also gave instructions for building healthy work relationships.

Getting Started

1. How do you define "family"?

2. What cultural attacks on the family have you observed recently?

Searching the Scriptures

Obey Your Parents

The opening verses of Ephesians 6 are important. They show that the Bible is relevant for children as well as adults. Paul did not command parents, "Teach these truths to your children" (although parents *should* teach Bible truths to their kids). He addressed the children directly. "Children, obey your parents in the Lord: for this is right," he wrote. The command to children does not read, "Obey your father" or "Obey your mother." It includes both parents. Even Jesus, the Son of God, subjected Himself to His earthly parents while He was growing up.

Children are to obey their parents "in the Lord." In other words, children should obey their parents because in doing so, they obey the Lord. No doubt Paul assumed that Christian parents would direct their children to do right.

3. What happens to the children who fail to make a connection between their obedience to their parents and their obedience to God?

Ephesians 6:1 does not address the issue of unsaved parents telling their children to do things contrary to God's will.

4. What should a young teenager do if his unsaved parents command him to stop reading the Bible?

5. What should a young child do if her parents forbid her to get baptized?

6. What should children do if their father tells them to lie to protect their family's reputation?

Honor Your Parents

Verse 2 goes beyond verse 1. Children should not only obey their parents, but they should also honor them. To honor them means to show them respect. It is possible to obey grudgingly. But honoring while obeying leaves no place for halfhearted obedience.

7. Read Ephesians 6:2. When, if ever, is a child free from the duty to honor his or her parents?

8. How does honoring their parents help children make right choices even when their parents are not around?

9. How can an adult child honor his or her parents?

A general promise comes with the command to honor one's parents: "That it may be well with thee, and thou mayest live long on the earth" (v. 3). Children who honor and obey their parents can look forward to a longer life on earth.

This promise has caused some questions, because Christian children do not always live longer than other children. How can we answer such a criticism? First, we must remember that this promise is a general truth. It does not mean every Christian child will live longer. Second, Christian children who honor and obey their Christian parents may not become involved in many of the world's vices, such as drugs and immorality. This lack of vices may cause them to live healthier, more productive lives.

When Paul promised, "that it may be well with thee" (v. 3), he included spiritual prosperity in the promise. Thus, the verse promises not only a longer life but a more blessed one as well. Furthermore, the blessings do not stop with this life, for rewards await obedient Christians in Heaven.

10. How important is it for a child to understand that his or her power to obey comes from the Spirit? (See Ephesians 5:18.)

Don't Provoke

Just as the husband-wife relationship is two-sided, so is the parent-child relationship. Children should obey their parents, and parents must not abuse their authority.

Paul discussed a negative aspect of parenting by writing, "And, ye fathers, provoke not your children to wrath" (Ephesians 6:4). Of course a mother as well as a father can provoke children by being uncomplimentary, overbearing, and impossible to please. A child may give up trying to please such a parent and turn away not only from the parent but from the Lord.

Parents who repeatedly ask their child, "Can't you do anything right?" should read and reread this verse until they no longer ask such a question. Likewise, parents should read and reread this verse if they ask their children to do things that lie beyond their ability. Parents should provide whatever their children need to obey—whether they need instructions on how to do something or tools to carry out the command. For example, before we ask our children to hang up their clothes, we should make sure we have provided hooks or hangers that they can reach so they are *able* to obey.

Biting criticism, unjust demands, and unreasonable severity have no rightful place in Christian parenting or, by extension, in Christian teaching. We should always remember that an ounce of praise goes a lot farther than a pound of criticism. Parents should aim to rear their children to love the Lord.

11. What does a child learn about God from watching and listening to his or her parents?

Nurture

Being too permissive is destructive too. Parents should not let their children rule the home. The Lord holds parents accountable to exercise loving discipline by setting reasonable guidelines and enforcing them. Paul instructed parents to bring up their children "in the nurture . . . of the Lord" (v. 4). The word "nurture" refers to discipline or chastening. It means "training that corrects, molds, and perfects moral character."

Children need discipline. They need molding to learn proper behavior, respect for authority, and getting along with others. They need to learn to behave at home, in school, in church, and in society. Discipline makes children better fit for life itself.

Parents must correct their children when they misbehave; however, parents should never attack their children in anger. If a parent is tempted to attack the child instead of lovingly dealing with the problem, he or she should wait awhile before disciplining the child. Furthermore, parents should never try to "get even" with a child after he or she has embarrassed the parents.

The punishment should always match the offense. Remember, too, that punishment is not an end in itself. It should correct the child so that in the future his or her behavior will change.

Admonition

Paul also instructed parents to bring up their children "in the . . . admonition of the Lord" (v. 4). Parents should teach their children how to live Biblically. This teaching might take place, in part, during family devotions. Certainly we should take time to read the Bible together. Small children can learn Bible stories and Biblical principles from children's Bible story books and from the Bible itself as parents read to them.

12. Besides formal instruction, how else can a parent teach his or her child? (See Deuteronomy 6:4–9.)

As children grow older and family schedules take members in different directions, carrying out this family-time instruction becomes more difficult. But we should make it a priority.

13. Why must a parent, like the child, know the truth of Ephesians 5:18?

14. Read 2 Timothy 1:2–5 and 3:15. What positive things can a grandparent do to help his or her grandchild grow spiritually?

Christian Employees

In Ephesians 6:5–9 Paul addressed servants and masters. In Paul's day people often considered their servants (slaves) to be part of the family. We are thankful that slavery has passed away in most parts of the world, but the principles Paul taught apply well to the current employer-employee relationship.

Believers should seek to do what their bosses ask them to do, not simply to please them, but to please the Lord Jesus Christ. We should work "as unto Christ" (v. 5).

15. Read Ephesians 6:5. What permission, if any, did Paul grant to the

Ephesian slaves to complain about their working conditions and owners?

16. What right, if any, do today's believers have to bad-mouth their bosses?

17. Read Ephesians 6:6. How should seeing Christ as a believer's ultimate boss change his or her work habits?

18. How do the truths and instructions in Ephesians 5:8 and 9 help an employee know how to respond at work?

Some Christians think that Christ will reward believers only for witnessing, studying the Bible, or doing things for their local church, but Ephesians 6:7 and 8 show that at the Judgment Seat of Christ, we will receive rewards for faithfulness on the job.

Christian Employers

Christian employers should treat their workers fairly. They should never threaten them (v. 9). They should pay them a just wage and should recognize that someday they will answer to Christ for how they treated their workers (v. 9).

19. Should a Christian employer ever fire someone? Explain.

20. How does a Christian boss's treatment of company policies affect his or her testimony?

We could summarize this whole section of Ephesians in two words: "Do right." Wives should do right; husbands should do right. Children should do right; parents should do right. Employees should do right, and employers should do right. If everyone heeded Paul's instructions in these verses, life would be far more enjoyable and less confrontational. God's Spirit makes it all possible (5:18).

Making It Personal

Because family relationships are so important and fragile, they should be handled with utmost care. Review your schedule from yesterday.

21. How did you relate to your family members? Were you kind in all your actions and remarks, or did you act and speak harshly at times? What did you do to help each family member become a stronger Christian?

22. What adjustments, if any, do you need to make today to relate better to each member of your family?

23. What will you do this week to strengthen your testimony in the workplace?

24. Memorize Ephesians 6:4 and 5 as a reminder to let God direct your relationships both in your home and at work.

Lesson 13

The Fight Is On and On and On

God enables the believer to withstand Satan's assault.

Ephesians 6:10–24

"Put on the whole armour of God, that ye may be able to stand against the wiles of the devil" (Ephesians 6:11).

H undreds of wars have raged throughout the centuries. Some lasted years, like the Hundred Years War, but others lasted only a short time. The shortest war on record took place between Great Britain and Zanzibar on August 27, 1896. It began shortly after 9:00 a.m. and ended before 10:00 a.m. In fact, it lasted only thirty-eight minutes. Zanzibar surrendered at 9:40 a.m. Needless to say, that war was also one of the least expensive ones in history!

The Christian must wage a war for the rest of his or her life, a war that demands constant preparedness and vigilance. The enemy is vile and vicious, and his tactics are often subtle. But every Christian can have victory over this enemy if he or she heeds the counsel that the apostle Paul gave in Ephesians 6:10–24.

1. Imagine being shot at by an unseen enemy. What thoughts would go through your mind?

2. What weapons and armor would you like to have at your disposal?

Paul began his final section of Ephesians by urging believers to "be strong in the Lord, and in the power of his might" (Ephesians 6:10). Paul knew the truth that Peter discovered the hard way: we cannot defeat the Devil by relying on our own strength.

3. Read Ephesians 6:10. Why can't the instructions in this verse be seen as optional?

4. What happens to the believer who is oblivious to Satan's desire to defeat him or her?

The Wily Enemy

Just as a soldier needs to know his enemy, the believer needs to know the Devil's characteristics, goals, and strategies. Satan is cunning and treacherous. He wants to dethrone God and destroy God's people, and he employs a wide variety of strategies as he attempts to accomplish his goals. So Paul instructed believers to dress in full armor in order to resist the "wiles" of the Devil (v. 11). "Wiles" refers to the Devil's craftiness, his deceitfulness, and his trickery.

5. Read 1 Peter 5:8. What do we learn about the Devil by comparing him to a roaring lion?

6. Read 2 Corinthians 11:14. How does this verse depict the Devil?

We must stay on guard, never relaxing our defenses. The Christian life is a constant warfare, and we will never retire from the Christian military. Satan and his angels are committed to obstructing the work of Christ moment by moment, day and night, week after week, and year after year. They hope to immobilize every Christian soldier.

7. Review Paul's instructions to the Ephesians in Ephesians 4:1—6:9. Which of the life issues that Paul covered in those chapters seem to be Satan's favorite battlefronts?

8. Do most Christians see everyday life issues as a place where Satan attacks? Why or why not?

The more effectively you live for Christ, the more savagely Satan will attack you. The story of the early church demonstrates this truth. The Devil attacked the apostles and other spiritual leaders furiously as they invaded his territory and proclaimed the gospel.

9. Read Acts 5:40 and 41 and 7:59 and 60. Who were targets of the Devil's fury? How did they respond?

The Armor

In Ephesians 6:11 Paul instructed believers to put on the "whole armour" of God. If we neglect even one piece, we become vulnerable to the Devil. We must be completely armed. The Devil knows our weak points, and he will aim for those spots. If he cannot bring us down one way, he will try another.

Satan's angels are organized into different ranks. Satan, the most powerful one, leads them. He is "the god of this world [age]" and "the prince of the power of the air" (2 Corinthians 4:4; Ephesians 2:2). The phrase "rulers of the darkness of this world" (Ephesians 6:12) refers to a group of high-ranking angels who follow the Devil. The term "against principalities, against powers" (v. 12) refers to angels belonging to other ranks in Satan's evil kingdom. Although we cannot see these evil spirit beings, they surround us.

Paul explained that our spiritual armor will enable us "to withstand in the evil day, and having done all, to stand" (v. 13).

The Belt, Breastplate, and Shoes

Paul described Christian soldiers prepared for battle as "having [their] loins girt about with truth" (v. 14). This description alludes to the kind of belt a Roman soldier put around his waist to keep all the other pieces of armor in place. Paul likened this belt to truth because the truth keeps everything in our lives in place.

10. Read John 8:44. What does this passage say about Satan?

11. What truths are important for believers to hold on to in the midst of battle?

12. What seemingly innocent lies does Satan want Christians to believe?

The breastplate covered the chest of the Roman soldier. A wound to the chest might have killed an unprotected soldier or at least removed him from battle. Paul exhorted believers to wear "the breastplate of righteousness" (Ephesians 6:14). This imagery pictures the Christian soldier leading a life of uprightness and integrity.

13. How vulnerable to Satan's attacks is a believer who is living a righteous life?

Roman soldiers wore thick-soled sandals with hobnails. Paul instructed us believers to have our "feet shod with the preparation of the gospel of peace" (v. 15). The shoes indicate the need to be prepared to tell the unsaved about the good news of peace with God through Jesus Christ.

14. How does the gospel provide peace for the Christian in the midst of battle?

15. Read Romans 10:13–15. How does this passage relate a believer's feet to the spread of the gospel message?

The Shield

In addition to his belt, breastplate, and shoes, a soldier valued his shield as an important part of his armor. He could hold it in his hand and turn it quickly to deflect arrows. In Paul's day, attackers used arrows not only to wound their opponents but also to burn them, for attackers would dip the ends of their arrows in tar and light them before shooting. Satan, too, uses "fiery darts" to inflict double damage if he succeeds in "hitting" us when our defenses are down (Ephesians 6:16). To defend ourselves against these darts, we must have faith, that is, a firm confidence in God and His Word.

16. Read Ephesians 6:16. What are some of the fiery darts that Satan may hurl at a believer?

The Helmet

Paul mentioned the helmet nearly last, but it is one of the most important parts of the armor. A severe blow to the head could bring sudden death. Paul likened the helmet to salvation. To be a soldier for Christ, a person must have believed on Christ as his or her personal Savior. But Paul probably had more than eternal salvation in mind when he wrote in verse 17, "And take the helmet of salvation," because he was writing to Christians. The Christian needs to have at least a basic knowledge of the teachings of the Bible. Christians must know in their own minds what the Bible teaches.

17. Read Ephesians 4:21. Paul took time to teach the Ephesians. How did Paul summarize what he taught them?

The Sword

God wants us not only to fight a defensive battle to hold our own against Satan and his demons but also to invade his territory. So Paul added an offensive weapon to his list of military equipment. He instructed us to take "the sword of the Spirit, which is the word of God" (6:17).

Sometimes a Roman soldier needed to take the offensive in a battle. Similarly, in the spiritual battle, we need to wield the sword of the Spirit, the Word of God, to strike down false beliefs. In seeking to win the lost from Satan's grasp, we need to take the offensive. We must have God's Word with us and use it to open the minds of those who need salvation (Romans 10:9–14; Hebrews 4:12). The Bible is an effective two-edged sword that enables us to cut down whatever opposition lies in our way as we advance with the gospel.

18. Read Ephesians 6:17. How can believers practically "take . . . the sword of the Spirit"?

Troop Support

Paul described believers as "praying always with all prayer" (Ephesians 6:18). But what is "all prayer"? We should pray for others; that kind of prayer is called intercession. We should also ask God to meet our needs—through a prayer called supplication. We may have fallen into sin and consequently must turn to God in repentance; we call that prayer confession. We may have received a blessing, so we thank Him for it in a prayer called praise and thanksgiving. To win battles over Satan, we should offer *all* the kinds of prayer.

19. Read Ephesians 6:18. How did Paul underscore the importance of prayer?

Paul taught sound doctrine, but he also applied it to life. So in typical fashion, he not only listed various kinds of prayer, but he also requested prayer for himself (v. 19). Although he was zealous and faithful, Paul knew he needed prayer. No one ever reaches a time when he or she no longer needs prayer.

20. Read Ephesians 6:19 and 20. Describe the openness that Paul, God's primary missionary of perhaps all time, used in requesting prayer for himself.

21. How does refusing to share our fears and struggles actually help the enemy gain ground in his battle against us?

Verses 21–24 close Paul's epistle to the Ephesians. The Ephesians loved Paul and would, of course, want to learn more about his situation. Paul had many faithful coworkers. Tychicus was one of them. So Paul told the Ephesians that Tychicus would bring them up to date when he visited them (v. 21).

In closing his letter, Paul also mentioned his desire that God would bless his readers with peace, love, faith, and grace (vv. 22–24). May God bless each of us in the same way as we apply what we have learned from Ephesians.

Making It Personal

The Scriptures and personal experience show clearly that we will face heated battles with Satan until we arrive in Heaven. But we are on the victory side, because Jesus, our Commander in Chief, supplies everything we need for the conflict.

22. Review the armor of God. Which pieces have you neglected to take up? By God's grace, take them up this week.

- the belt of truth
- the breastplate of righteousness
- the shoes of the gospel of peace
- the shield of faith
- the helmet of salvation

23. How have you been swinging your sword lately? What will you do to sharpen your skills with it this week?

24. How will you change your prayer habits so you can support your fellow troops better?

25. Memorize Ephesians 6:11 as a reminder to be aware of Satan's wily ways.